JOHN RAY

CYCLING TODAY

AN INSTRUCTIVE GUIDE TO THE NEW REVIVAL

Author: *John Ray*
Photographer: *Philip Sayer*
Managing Editors: *Errol Drew, Brian Stewart*

Madison Books

CYCLING TODAY

AN INSTRUCTIVE GUIDE TO THE NEW REVIVAL

Contents

ISBN 0 9509552 0 5

Printed and bound in Great Britain for Madison Books, a division of Madison Cycles Ltd, Unit 7, Oxgate Lane, London NW2 7HT by Presscraft, Hartlebury Printers Ltd, Unit 111D, Hartlebury, Near Kidderminster, Worcs DY10 4JB.

Introduction

I feel obliged to admit at the outset that I am one of those people who only learned to ride a bicycle as an adult. Should this make you, the reader, feel rather like a hospital patient who has just learned that his surgeon only became qualified last week, I should add that I have since more than made up for the late start. In addition, I began my cycling career free from all those childhood associations which often tend to cloud the issue for adults - associations which, in the UK at least, tend to recall sturdy British brand names and nostalgically low prices expressed in pounds, shillings and pence.

Stripped of nostalgia the bicycle remains a brilliant invention, a superbly efficient method of transport and a unique source of enjoyment - for anyone.

Cycling today is better than ever before because the machines are better than ever before. The new revival has brought with it a generation of cyclists many of whom, just a few years ago, would never have dreamed of buying and using a bike costing two or three hundred pounds.

This book is addressed to those who in one way or another have caught the flavour of the new revival. It may be that you already spend a lot of time on a good bike. It may be that you're only thinking of buying a modern bike. Either way, this is not the place to look for comic-strip instructions on how to mend a puncture, or for romantic passages about cycling into the sunset equipped only with a groundsheet and a lightweight copy of Wordsworth's sonnets. My intention is rather to explore those aspects of cycling which tend to get people started and then to proceed through improvement (of both rider and machine) to top quality bikes and equipment. Sometimes I have tried to suggest a new approach to this or that aspect of cycling. This is not because the subject needs novelty but because I still find that many people, for whom a bike is an object familiar since childhood, are bound by old prejudice and seem unable to appreciate the abundant possibilities offered by the new revival.

Of course I am offering a personal viewpoint throughout. My own prime interest in cycling is in using it as an extension of city life. Your own experience and conclusions are unlikely to coincide exactly with mine. This is as it should be. I hope at least that we agree that the bicycle has been left rusting in the shed for too long. The time has come to get it out, inspect it carefully and then throw it away and buy a new one.

Chapter One

Revival

The meeting of old ideas and new machines.

A few years ago a friend of mine acquired a bicycle free of charge. It was at once clear that this was the most he expected to pay. It was a strange-looking bike and I remember thinking at the time that the wheels were either of some highly specialised design or else had come off a pram. My friend was disappointed to discover that he would have to buy new tyres. Days of anxiety and indecision followed as he worried about spending considerably less than the weekly bus fare which he would no longer have to pay. In the end he bought one tyre and shortly afterwards had both wheels stolen. This marked the end of his cycling career. To have paid out even more on a lock had of course been quite out of the question.

The odd thing about his behaviour is that, at the time no one thought it odd. To act in this strange, pennypinching and illogical way was alright because - well, it was only a bike. In much the same spirit, comedians used to tell jokes in which the bicycle always featured as the poor man's transport - the comic contrast to someone else's flashy sportscar. The same comedians probably still tell these jokes but the point of them has now vanished. The revival is now well established and probably permanent. At its heart is the surge of technological improvement which has quite suddenly turned a classic invention into a sublime one. Virtually every single component of a bicycle can now be made better in all respects than ever before. The same can be said of many other inventions, but never with quite the same implications. The responsiveness of a machine which depends exclusively on your own physical effort and dexterity, is uniquely improved by strong, light and precisely engineered parts.

There are other variable factors which have contributed to the new revival - an increasing preoccupation with physical fitness, the deterioration of public transport, the congestion of towns and cities - but the basic and continuing appeal lies in the simplicity of the original invention now amplified and refined in today's high quality cycles.

It may be that you are not yet quite ready to think of bicycles in these positive terms. If so I don't want to put you off with overblown enthusiasm and so I shall begin with a gentle introduction for newcomers.

You, as a newcomer, may, like many others, think of bikes rather like cars - that is to say standard units, ready-built with only limited possibilities for variation: colour, extras etcetera. This is not so. It is left up to whoever happens to be combining the various components - frame, wheels, brakes, saddle, chainset and so on - as to how things turn out. When the motivation is exclusively profit, then some very odd items can be offered for sale. Department and chain stores are usually the worst offenders although often as a result of ignorance rather than profiteering. Whatever the reason, you don't want to be riding around on the chance result of some shrewd business deal struck between the UK and Korea, anymore than you want to be sold your bike by someone who is normally serving on soft toys. Go to a cycle dealer. He ought to be able to cater for the most well-informed cyclist as well as the newcomer, although it would be unrealistic to pretend that a busy cycle shop is the best place to do your initial research if you are not too familiar with basics. If you retain a hazy childhood notion of "racers" as opposed to "ordinary" bikes, or feel that ten gears sound like seven too many for your simple tastes, then clarification is necessary before getting down to cases.

Three speed bikes with heavy frames, trigger gear-change, straight handlebars and plastic saddles complete with cartoon springs are fine as far as they go ... which is to say about twenty miles - thirty if you're tough. Like any offspring of limited ability, such a bike is often fondly defended by its owner, but the fact remains that it is totally inferior to the kind of cycle we are concerned with here. This is why a bike like the one pictured on the cover of this book (in common with all five and ten-speed bikes) uses derailleur gears which are mechanically more efficient than three-speed hub gears. The numbers five and ten - sometimes more - indicate a range of possibilities rather than a strict sequence of steps. The bike has drop handlebars which when correctly adjusted make for a more efficient riding position. The unsprung saddle would only be an uncomfortable alternative if you tried to sit upright on it; as it is the shape and design contribute to the overall comfort of the forward cycling position where a proportion of the rider's body weight is transferred to the arms. Finally, the lightweight frame is in no way an insubstantial version of the solid old roadster, as it is not only lighter but stronger and more resilient as well. These basic distinctions are here simply stated since they are well known to experienced cyclists. But I think they are well worth pointing out because so often they are taken as read by those in the know, leaving newcomers with the vague impression that there is something flashy and pretentious about "racing" bikes which somehow exceeds their imagined requirements. Oddly enough, this impression is often reinforced when a rider accustomed to a heavy bike first tries out a good one. The unfamiliar feel of a light, responsive machine can be unsettling to someone used to trudging around on a solid one - the bike appears to have a will of its own. Nothing can be done except to point out that experience shows that after a couple of weeks on a good lightweight bike, a return to the old faithful would be unthinkable.

This said, I freely admit that bicycles of all shapes and sizes and in all states of repair have given enjoyment and often essential transport to millions of people the world over. When making fine distinctions between good and bad bicycle design one can't help but wonder how it is that the entire population of China seems to have got it wrong. The answer I suppose is that such a classic invention will withstand all sorts of design and manufacturing oddities and unless a given bike actually collapses it may give satisfaction until compared with something better.

Incidental descriptions of bicycle rides crop up in all sorts of books and I particularly like this simple account of an evening ride which took place, as it happens, in Vyra, Russia, in 1911:

"I had turned upside down and lowered to subsaddle level the handlebars of my Enfield bicycle, converting it into my conception of a racing model. Along the paths of the park I would skim, following yesterday's patterned imprint of Dunlop tires; neatly avoiding the ridges of tree roots; selecting a fallen twig and snapping it with my sensitive front wheel; weaving between two flat leaves and then between a small stone and the hole from which it had been dislodged the evening before; enjoying the brief smoothness of a bridge over a brook; skirting the wire fence of the tennis court; nuzzling open the little whitewashed gate at the end of the park ... ." *

* "Speak, Memory" by Vladimir Nabokov.

It would be foolish to suppose that the ride so described was at all impaired by a heavy and amateurishly modified machine. The experience itself counted. Even so, people's expectations of technology are today extremely high and it is in this context that acceptable limits of bicycle manufacture should be considered. Certainly my recommendation for a bicycle which meets the minimum standards necessary to give you a degree of cycling satisfaction, would cost you in the region of two hundred pounds. (Two hundred pounds is what you pay for a year's worth of commuting at forty pence each way, five days a week.) For this sort of outlay you could expect to get the following:

1. A lightweight frame made from highgrade steel alloy tubing. Externally this is indistinguishable from the cheapest tubing but the difference in "feel" is total; the better frame will be light and responsive in use and to a certain extent, capable of absorbing road shock. In the absence of suspension this factor is most important as is the quality of the front forks which bear the brunt of any sudden impact.

2. Wheels with alloy rims fitted with good quality, reliable tyres.

3. An alloy chainset with forged crank arms and detachable rings. This enables you to change the range of gears available to you - or replace worn rings - without the unnecessary expense of a new chainset.

4. A gearing system of reliable manufacture designed to cover a wide range of ratios suitable for all sorts of terrain.

5. Other components (with spares availability) from manufacturers with established reputations. Some reliable brand names to look out for are S.R. & Miche for pedals and hubs; Weinmann & Red S for brakes; Madison for saddles; Shimano, Huret & Suntour for gears.

If you are about to buy a bike and are feeling cautious about money, the large number of makes and models in this price range can make the choice bewildering. The Revell Ritmo is one good example of the quality I would recommend as a beginner's cycle for someone who intends to have a serious attempt at experiencing what modern cycling is all about. Whilst none of its components is anywhere near the top of the range, all have been thoughtfully chosen and combined, and for a basic minimum bike, its level of performance is very high. Worthy of special note is the fact that not only the main frame but also the front forks and rear stays are made from lightweight tubing. This careful approach is reflected throughout, the underlying attitude being one of informed design balanced against cost. As such it is an attitude very much a part of the new status enjoyed by cycling. Of course, there are other models that would serve equally as well, but I would recommend you solicit the advice of an experienced cyclist or better still a knowledgeable cycle dealer, a selection of whom are listed in the back of this book.

The best cycle dealers used to be either specialists catering for cliques of competition enthusiasts, or else good-natured old men willing to spend an unprofitable afternoon mending the district nurse's puncture without the aid of their reading glasses. There was and is a place for both types of service, but the kind of dealer who appeals to today's new cyclist stocks and sells (and sometimes designs) machines which raise the expectations of his customer and then satisfies those expectations.

Chapter Two

Handling Heavy Traffic

Techniques for mastering city roads.

The highway code is an excellent little book and, treated as fiction can do no harm at all. However any cyclist who imagines that motorised road users are going to behave according to its instructions are going to be sadly - perhaps dangerously - disappointed. This is not to suggest that our roads are dominated by homicidal maniacs - just people. It is helpful to reflect that among those in charge of motor vehicles are failed insurance salesmen, retired fire-engine drivers, defrocked bishops, women on their way back from pregnancy tests, men in rally jackets, drunks, Frenchmen and someone who has reached third gear without realising that the Krooklok is still attached. These people may have things on their mind other than your safety. Since the standard of bike-riding is generally even lower than the standard of car-driving, it must be clear that I am not pointing the finger at any one group - it's up to you to survive *and* enjoy biking in town.

Clearly lack of attention is fatal. You may just be one of the few people who cannot concentrate properly on driving or cycling. Symptoms of this condition are having lots of accidents and the cure is to stop doing it at once. As for the rest of us, my feeling is that while we are waiting for those Utopian cycle paths, mixing with motorised traffic is a skill to be learned and which, once learned, is actually exciting and enjoyable to practise.

Being seen is your first requirement. This involves positioning yourself on the road so that other people can see you - a discreet course close to the kerb is not necessarily a good thing. An example would be the cyclist who suddenly finds his way blocked by a stationary bus and pulls out into the path of a car which is also about to overtake the bus. This may or may not be OK - it depends on whether the driver is momentarily distracted, his rate of acceleration, and so on. In any case a potentially dangerous moment has occurred. Better for the cyclist to have pulled out much earlier and blocked the car's path until both had passed the obstruction. The car driver may find this frustrating, but that potentially dangerous moment has been anticipated and avoided. The driver cannot in fact justifiably complain - he is sharing the road with the cyclist, probably at less risk of personal injury, and must share the inconvenience of this unsatisfactory state of affairs. The sort of situation described above usually happens to me two or three times a day and therefore is easily recognised and dealt with. Of course most tricky traffic situations are by their nature unpredictable and things can happen fast. It is precisely these factors which make for enjoyable cycling once you are confident and skillful enough to join in the game. This is not to be flippant nor is it to minimise very real danger, it is simply acknowledging that any athletic activity which involves speed and competition and split-second judgement is exciting when done well.

I have indicated that the cyclist's traditional text-book role is irrelevant to today's city cyclist. I cannot advise you to overtake on the inside or ride on the pavement or break the law in other ways; I can only say that if it is a safer alternative you would be foolish not to. You are then obliged to proceed with more than due caution. There are places where "No Cycling" paths offer tempting alternatives to dangerous intersections. Cyclists who choose these routes of course annoy park keepers ... and there are those who might feel that this is justification in itself. Sensible authorities provide cycle routes through their parks - an exercise requiring only a bucket of white paint and the ability to spell the word "Bicycles".

Militancy on the road itself is usually a mistake. It is stupid to insist on your imagined right when competing with a truck driver who is intent on reaching Turin with minimum use of his brakes. If you can't safely get where you want to be in fast traffic, pull over and wait - five minutes if necessary.

Just as riding next to the kerb confers no automatic safety, travelling at minimum speed will not make you immortal. When you get good enough you may find that travelling faster in traffic is a lot safer than creeping along. For a start, your speed relative to traffic going in the same direction, will actually decrease, making manoeuvres easier and more clearly visible to everyone. On the other hand, jubilant cyclists hurtling through traffic jams are highly vulnerable. Sometime, somewhere a car door will open.

In heavy traffic you should certainly wear some sort of protective headgear. Helmets made specifically for cyclists are getting better all the time, and the Skid-Lid actually looks quite good, if appearance bothers you unduly. The Hanna Pro, Kiwi and the Max are less expensive but very lightweight helmets and any of these are recommended. Reluctance to use a helmet is understandable but more or less indefensible. It may be inconvenient and only of use in circumstances that most people do not want to dwell on, but I suspect that unfamiliarity is the most off-putting thing. The same was true of motorcycle helmets, but even before legislation made them compulsory in Britain, their use had become widespread and, once accepted, they were generally seen as a sensible piece of equipment. You always have the option to forget the helmet when riding in the country or when the weather is just too hot, but for mixing with traffic, wear one.

Recommended Cycling Helmets

Max
Very light. Approx. price £15.00.

Kiwi
Comfortable, but somewhat heavier with less ventialtion than the others, this make is more attractive than most. It claims to exceed a proposed International standard on cycle helmet protection.
Approx. price £26.00.

Hanna Pro
This helmet uses an unusual fitting arrangement so that it can be adjusted to fit any shape of head. There is also a children's size version.
Approx. price £29.00.

Skid Lid
Quite different in appearance to all the others, its open star shaped top design saves weight and offers excellent ventilation. I also like its other thoughtful touches like the washable chamois forehead liner and clip-on rear view mirror.
Approx. price £39.00.

Chapter Three

Freedom of the City

Useful hints on urban commuting.

Commuting by bike is not a task but something I positively enjoy. On the rare occasions that circumstances force me to travel by public transport in the rush hour, I am always astonished that so many fairly fit-looking people submit themselves to this dismal ritual of daily disenchantment. For anyone with a reasonable distance to travel, good co-ordination and common sense, a bike almost always proves itself a far superior solution to the problem of travelling to work. The money you save can be considerable, but traditional worries persist: rain, lights, carrying luggage.

Well, yes, it will rain - and wet weather used to be a big problem. Quite apart from the discomfort, no one wants to arrive at their destination looking as if they've fallen in the river. Those yellow capes have always been something of a mixed blessing - more or less OK until a quirky gust of wind blows the thing inside out over your head and you coast to destruction like a giant daffodil. The best solution is to equip yourself with garments made from Goretex such as the Caldo range of cycling clothing. These products are so good it's difficult to sound objective about them. Completely waterproof, windproof, very light, breathable and well-styled, they are manufactured expressly for the cyclist. The fabric used is waterproof yet breathes like a natural fabric to allow body moisture to evaporate. The inescapable conclusion I have come to, is that a Caldo suit is infinitely better than a cape. It is also more expensive than a cape. In fact it is more expensive than several capes but should be considered as standard equipment. If you decide that a cape is what you want, then Pakit is probably the best choice. Whatever you choose though, get something that works, because you cannot cycle safely in town or anywhere, if you are cold and wet.

Making sure that you are visible to other road users at night is the most important safety precaution you can take. A number of new lighting systems have recently appeared which, in varying degrees, overcome the serious limitations of those previously available. Of these the Byka Electronic Lamp is the most advanced

I've seen. Within the front lamp is a unit which switches automatically between generator and battery depending upon the power being generated from the dynamo. It is more expensive than ordinary lamps of course but this is not an area in which it is worth cutting costs in my opinion.

In general, the fundamental choice in lights is between dynamo and battery powered systems. If you are going to be mean or sloppy about replacing low batteries, you had better use a dynamo. The Sanyo Dynapower and Byka generators which fit inconspicuously behind the bottom bracket and run on the middle of the rear tyre are probably the best bet at the time of writing. The Byka generator has the advantage of not slipping when wet. If you prefer battery lights then you'll find that the Slimlite front and rear lamps are bright, lightweight and can be easily removed when leaving your bike unattended.

If you ride a bike in traffic, day or night, you should wear a reflective Sam Browne belt, a safety aid which is well on the way to becoming established as *the* symbol denoting a two-wheeled vehicle. Be sure that the one you choose is made from Reflexite which is a highly visible fabric that may quite literally turn out to be a lifesaver, especially if your lights fail at a crucial moment.

You will need to leave your bike unattended in town - maybe even all day outside your place of work. There seems to me little point in always carrying a lock and conscientiously using it if the thing is going to offer minimal resistance to any thief over the age of ten. If you are going to leave your bike in town and wish to do so with confidence, buy yourself a Citadel lock. These U-shaped hardened metal locks represent a powerful deterrent to the would-be thief and have earned their reputation as the ultimate cycle lock.

So, protected against the weather, reasonably conspicuous to other road users and in with a chance of finding your bike where you left it, you are free to enjoy some of the advantages of city cycling. The approach described in the previous chapter assumes the busiest kind of city traffic; however, things are frequently much quieter. In any town you can get through narrow gaps in traffic, thread yourself through motionless queues or even get off and walk when everything comes to a standstill. You can often maintain a higher average speed than most motor vehicles and park more or less anywhere. These advantages are available to almost any cyclist, whatever the level of skill.

As to the bike itself, a good quality basic machine, as outlined in chapter one, will work as well in town as anywhere. The basic standards of safety and performance are for all-round use, but you may want to set up your bike for optimum results in the kind of situation you most often encounter. This is covered more fully in a later chapter. More pressing for many people are practical considerations like carrying luggage - books, shopping, children. Rear panniers (rigid boxes or shaped bags) offer the most convenient form of instantly detachable containers. The advent of a very tough lightweight board - Correx - has made possible the manufacture of rigid panniers which weigh little more than nylon bags. Called "Bicase", these panniers are the only choice for anyone wanting to carry fragile items or books without adding significantly to the weight of the bike. Bags can be a bit fiddly and shapeless when empty but have the advantage of letting you throw in sundry articles which rigid panniers might not easily accept - for example, two kilos of potatoes or a small accordion (Well, you might ... !). Anyway, the weight is kept low, so aiding stability, and the rear carrier which you will need to support the panniers can be used on its own for the attachment of other bags or small loads. If you want to travel ultra-light you can use the handy little Pakit pouch which straps under the saddle and will hold a spare tube and a toolkit and not much else. The slightly larger Pakit seat pack could even accommodate a rainwear article together with a compressed ryebread sandwich. A fuller examination of the wide variety of bags and carriers available appears in the chapter dealing with touring equipment.

If you want to carry a child on the back of your bike then the Safe-Ride child seat will carry a child weighing up to 18 kilograms. Mounted over the rear wheel it comes complete with a guard to prevent inquisitive infants from seeing what happens when they put their feet in the spokes.

A word about tyres in general and punctures in particular. I assume that you will not be considering tubular tyres for town use; their design and characteristics make them ideal for competition but inappropriate for practical use. There is a wide range of wire-on tyres available (wire-ons are simply the traditional type: tyres with a wire bead which take an inner tube) and, within the limitations of your rims, you may care to experiment with them. Depending on your use and loading of the bike you might prefer a heavier type (with subsequent loss of response) to a lighter faster one. Nutrak produce a superb range of high-performance tyres which cover the widest range of requirements. The appropriate one for your rims and and usage should be selected. Used in conjunction with a product unpromisingly called "Mr Tuffy Tape" these tyres may even give you many months of puncture-free cycling on glass-strewn city streets.

"Mr Tuffy Tape" is in fact an extruded polymer ribbon which when inserted between tyre and inner tube prevents all but the most vicious objects from penetrating the tube. Having commuted with and without this tape I can informally endorse its claim to prevent a high percentage of punctures. It isn't the complete answer but goes most of the way to eliminating a big problem. Its effect on the handling of the bike is minimal and its cost fairly soon recouped in savings on irreparable inner tubes, not to mention time and trouble. This product may however have been overtaken by the introduction of the new Beltguard range by Nutrak. These tyres incorporate a flexible puncture resistant layer built in giving a lighter alternative without the problem of fitting an extra component.

Finally, a small gadget that I managed very well without for years has now established itself as a permanent addition to my around-town bike - the Mirrycle rear-view mirror. Despite the disadvantage of sounding as if it was named by the same man who thought up "Mr Tuffy", this is a very good product. Being tough, light and cleverly designed to look like an extension of the brake-lever assembly, it's a very reassuring little extra when you're in heavy traffic, particularly at night.

The last thing I want to do is leave you with the impression that cycling in town is fraught with problems - I have just tried to indicate that some sort of solution exists for any difficulty you may encounter. Also, today's solutions are nearly always improving and updating themselves by virtue of new technology and the enterprising nature of the modern cycle trade. The main thing is to enjoy the benefits, and enjoyment of city cycling has recently been enhanced by the arrival of the All Terrain or Mountain Bikes. Although intended initially for rough off-road riding, a good ATB like the Ridgeback, can be pressed into service quite happily for town use. Their sense of control, comfort and ruggedness combines with superior braking power to give a really good ride on city streets. Carrying heavy loads is easy, kerb-hopping is a lot of fun and the more upright riding position is of positive advantage in traffic. Recent trends towards supplying slightly narrower tyres than those intended for off-road riding indicate that the ATB may end up a permanent part of the urban cycling scene.

Recommended Equipment

Goretex Rainwear
The Caldo range is obviously designed for cycling but I frequently use my Shoreline model jacket at other times. I particularly like this jacket for its foldaway hood collar and ventilating zips under the arms. Another advantage is the high visibility light grey colour.
Caldo jacket prices range from £35 to £100 depending on the style you choose, and the overtrousers cost around £35.00.

Pakit Cape
This is a durable make in a tough rubber-backed nylon fabric. It includes a well designed hood and vents in the back.
Approx. price £17.00.

Byka Lighting System
Aided by a halogen front light and brighter than normal rear lamp this is probably the brightest cycle lighting system available. Sold either as a complete system or in various combinations of units.

Pakit Pouch
A neat nylon bag that can be fastened under the saddle to carry spare tubes, repair kit and essential tools.
Approx. price £3.00

Pakit Seatpack
A more substantial saddle bag similar to the pouch.
Approx. price £17.50

Sam Browne Belt
This should be made from the plastic Reflexite fabric which is highly visible both day and night. I like the simple snap-shut buckle found on the Bike Brite brand.
Approx. price £5.50.

Citadel Locks
There are two versions available in differing sizes, both offering the same high level of security, but I prefer the Model 2 series with the hollow key which I have found more convenient to operate. Citadel also make a neat nylon bracket to carry the lock on your bike.
Approx. price of lock £20.00, bracket £4.00.

Bicase Panniers
Most convenient for commuting use,these panniers are made from a remarkably light yet tough material called Correx. Some shops sell them as singles.
Approx. price £9.50 each.

Safe Ride Child Seat
I like the allround protection of the high back and sides as well as the padded grab rail.
Approx. price £24.00.

Mr Tuffy Tape
This comes in various sizes for different sized tyres. It's worth checking occasionally to ensure that the tape is properly seated between the tyre and the tube.
Approx. price £6.50 per pair.

Nutrak Tyres
Their new Marathon model is probably the best allround cycle tyre I have seen. It is available in both the wider 700 x 32c size as well as 27 x 1¼. (The Beltguard version has a puncture proof layer built into the tyre).
Approx. price £6.50, with Beltguard £12.00.

Mirrycle
A rear view mirror that is indispensible in city traffic on a cycle with drop handlebars.
Approx. price £7.00.

Ridgeback All Terrain Cycle
There are three models with different frame qualities and component specifications.
Prices range from £230.00 to £345.00.

Chapter Four

Branching Out

Cycling for the fun of it.

Somewhere between the routine ride to work and the epic tour of the Himalayas is a whole area of possibilities for the cyclist. As my own enthusiasm for biking around increased I found that I was beginning to make trips, in an evening or at a weekend, which were pleasant, not strictly necessary and which I would not have considered if car, motorcycle or public transport had been required. The informality of the bicycle combined with the enjoyment of the ride itself made the most casual digressions worthwhile - an unfamiliar bit of the city, countryside or whatever became worth a visit since getting there was at least half of the fun. In some cases getting there was all of the fun since by its nature exploring can result in disappointment as well as revelation; this is neither here nor there, the point is that quite soon a good bike makes you want to go and ride it. I am told of cases where commuting cyclists have even changed jobs for the sole reason that they will have further to cycle to work. Whilst I personally think that this is overdoing it, certainly I have sought out every feasible alternative to my regular routes and once or twice have been unable to resist the temptation of making an unnecessary circuit of the Outer Circle in Regents Park, despite having taken the road as a short cut in the first place.

Once you have crossed the threshold and come to recognise your bike for what it can do for you if you have the imagination to use it, you will come to look at personal transport in a quite different way. Of course the advantages of motorised transport are undeniable and I would not for a moment suggest that you abandon all uses of this in favour of cycling - I simply recommend that you should approach the decision of how to travel on a given journey from the assumption that a journey by bike can be positively pleasurable in itself. There may be such a thing as a pleasurable bus journey but for me at least, it's a difficult concept to grasp. If you can educate yourself into making travelling as much of a pleasure as arriving, then it follows that you will want to give both aspects of an outing equal consideration.

An enjoyable aspect of this sort of cycling is that one can travel light. Usually the best thing to do is to take as little as you need - a light toolkit and rainwear in a smallish seat pack and maybe a stuffsac (a cylindrical nylon bag) which can be packed down small for use only if things are acquired en route. A good bike should then be equally at home in town or country. It will only let you down if you feel an irresistible urge to plunge across fields and up mountains. Try it sometime on your super lightweight narrow-section tyre bike, and then wish you hadn't! This particular gap in the bicycle's abilities was noted in the USA where rough tracks and poorly maintained roads in some rural areas prompted the development of all-terrain bikes - very strong, lightweight cycles with balloon tyres for traction, wide straight handlebars for control and gearing capable of letting you ride up a steepish flight of stairs without undue effort. The overall appearance of one of these bikes is one of robust sturdiness and yet they are surprisingly light. They invite comparison with kids' BMX bikes although they are in nearly all cases far better made and intended for all types of tough practical use, not just flashy acrobatics. If you think the comparison with kids' stuff is off-putting, I can only recount the reaction of some ten year-olds who saw me riding my Ridgeback in London traffic; "Look," said one to the other, "he's got a real one!" Obviously they had harboured a vague suspicion all along that their BMXs were imitations of some authentic original they had never actually seen. Of course matched part for part with a quality racing cycle, Ridgebacks and other good all-terrain bikes compare unfavourably for lightness and speed. But as alternative bikes for taking to the country they open up enormous possibilities for enjoyment that have never been available before and which may in fact be the only attraction of cycling for some people. I was unconvinced of the need for such bikes in the UK until I tried one and found that in fact they are enormous fun. And I shall use mine gratefully in town whenever the road surfaces are slippery with snow or sleet because the brakes and tyres together recall motorcycle stopping power and control. Better all-terrain bikes are built to last as well as being plain good fun to ride and it would not surprise me to see them become widely popular and the natural successors to the old style roadsters, upgraded in every way and bringing rough roads and tracks within reach of every cyclist.

This informal kind of enjoyment that bikes offer has particular appeal for me. Touring also has its appeal, but I find somehow that touring is something you are going to do next summer, or did the year before last - in short, you don't do it all that often. These little trips and weekend jaunts I have been suggesting can take place anytime, most of the year round without planning or major equipping. They expand the use you can make of your bike and open up areas of recreation not available to anyone else.

A combination of bicycle and other types of transport means that you can go cycling in unfamiliar places often quite far away, without the full commitment of a cycle tour. Excellent racks are available for attaching one or several bikes to cars and vans.

Another alternative is to take your bike by train to wherever takes your fancy. For the cyclist, as for everyone else, British Rail is a mixed blessing. I feel obliged to strike this cautionary note, although generally my own experience of taking a bike by train has been good. Certainly the advantages are considerable if everything goes well - a day return to a distant town which you can then see by bike is certainly a bargain when the bike goes free. On the other hand, if you and the bike go to different towns much of the advantage is lost. At the time of writing the procedure is this: bikes are carried at the discretion of the guard - my experiences in this respect have all been good, although some regions are better than others. There is no charge for your bike unless your journey involves a 125 train - on these trains the guardsvan is small and a charge (half fare) is presumably levied to discourage cyclists altogether; in any case three bikes in one of these vans would probably involve evicting the guard. You are required to label your bike with your name and destination. Hardly anyone bothers to do this which is foolish since there is then no way of telling the cyclist that his steed is about to be uncoupled and left in a siding. Bikes are not allowed on busy commuter routes and certain other trains, usually for quite good reasons. Generally, the advantages far outweigh the snags and once you have ironed out the wrinkles - spotting the guardsvan as the train pulls in for a two minute stop is one of these, negotiating connecting services another - free bike transportation opens up a whole new range of cycling opportunities.

You may wish to explore the more competitive side of riding in which case you should contact The British Cycling Federation who will give you the name of your nearest cycling club. If you decide to join a club don't be put off by the sophisticated equipment and general atmosphere of knowledgeable enthusiasm as this quickly becomes less formidable as you participate and get to know the other members. The kind of activities generally offered can be briefly summarised here.

Club runs
These are usually Sunday rides divided into fast and easy groups which meet up half-way at a pub or some other appropriate place and then split up again.

Reliability trials
Here participants attempt to cover a certain distance in a predetermined time as a check on fitness and reliability. These are not races.

Road races
Club members accumulate points and are classified accordingly into three grades of ability. There are also veteran and junior categories. Races on the open road are either within the club or against a rival club. Tactics and team work can play a major role.

Time trials
Distances of ten, twenty, fifty and a hundred miles are covered by competitors setting off at regular intervals. Fastest time wins.

Track racing
Less popular, this involves both a track bike and the availability of a track. Exciting stuff for enthusiasts though.

Longer meetings, for example a week or long weekend, take place throughout the year for those who want fast touring or training holidays, and various social events, such as club dinners etcetera, enable you to mix with like-minded enthusiasts.

However you choose to spend your cycling time, you may find every now and again that you are overtaken by cycle tourists, They are equipped with artfully arranged pannier systems, water bottles, handlebar bags - tents, even. They probably exceeded your afternoon's mileage before breakfast. The next chapter suggests ways of approaching it and how you might equip yourself.

500m

Godfrey Davis

Transporting Bicycles On Cars

Elite San Remo
Alloy cross rails require cars with conventional gutters for attachment. Up to four cycles can be carried, clamped by their front forks with the front wheel removed.
Approx. price for two cycles £50.00.

A.M. Cycle Carrier
Cycles rest on two arms which are suspended on the boot or tailgate of the car. The lower operating level makes handling easier and offers less wind resistance than on a roof carrier. Up to two bikes.
Approx. price £25.00.

Addresses

British Cycling Federation
16 Upper Woburn Place
London WC1

Professional Cycling Association
4 Lane Top
Queensbury
Bradford
West Yorkshire

RESTAURANT
BAR
L'ébréché

Chapter Five

Open Roads

Touring, camping, exploring.

Some years ago a friend and his wife made full and comprehensive plans to go cycling in France. Crossings were booked, purpose-made clothing bought and panniers packed to capacity. Their imminent departure caused quite a stir in the street as the equipment was assembled and a small crowd gathered to see them leave. They set off amid cheers but before reaching the end of the street one of the wheels collapsed. All there was time to do was to fling the wreckage indoors, take a taxi to Waterloo and use up the tickets. Later, aboard the ferry, dressed in shorts and cycling shoes and carrying panniers they were approached by other cyclists anxious to know what machines they had, what gearing ratios they preferred and how many miles they expected to cover. "Well, actually ..." the explanation began.

This sort of experience is clearly a case of practical considerations being swept aside in the general enthusiasm and it is easy to understand. Much of the pleasure associated with touring lies in the planning. With Ordnance Survey map spread out at home you can anticipate your achievements in complete comfort - storming up steep hills, striking out north, south, east or west as the whim takes you, covering five or even six-and-a-half inches a day without discomfort. You can spend days, weeks even, deciding what accessories to buy, wavering between settling for an ultra lightweight survival kit or catering for every possible comfort - which packs down to about the size of a polar expedition supplies sledge.

The tour itself will undoubtedly hold a few surprises, but it is this unpredictable nature of cycle touring that makes it so appealing. Of course you can pursue your chosen route with dogged persistence and with no regard for terrain or prevailing wind or any miscalculation of your own powers, but there is little point in it. The charm of cycle touring is the freedom it offers. I found it a good idea to start with a short tour to gauge my capabilities, and then to try something more ambitious. I suggest you find your natural level of performance and then plan accordingly. Touring is in fact quite unique in that your appreciation of distance travelled changes during the course of the day's ride. The initial twenty miles always feel as if they take longer than the subsequent forty or fifty. One settles into a rhythm during the course of the day and so a day spent touring acquires a shape of its own. Experience allows you to plan a day's cycling and destination with confidence and also to depart from any plan and use a map to investigate interesting things on the way.Once again the rail system can be incorporated into your travels to cut out boring stretches. This raises the question of why exactly you go touring. What is boring for one person may interest another and if you are going with someone else you should make sure that you are in general agreement about the type of trip you envisage.Head-down mile-eaters do not travel well with casual meanderers. The accessibility of France is a considerable plus for the British cyclist. It is cheap to get there, enormously varied when you arrive and the bicycle enjoys the kind of status you would expect from a civilised country. And of course you can go as far as you wish - a complete European tour if the fancy takes you. Another advantage is that in general the cyclist is treated with more consideration on the roads of Europe.

The importance of suitable gearing cannot be overstated. If your lowest gear is inadequate for steep hills when your bike is lightly laden, it will certainly be useless when you're fully equipped. Touring is not a survival test - it's supposed to be enjoyable, so you should experiment with loading and gearing your bike before departure if possible. A good guide is to try your steepest local incline fully laden. You should be able to pedal up any hill without dismounting. For two riders unevenly matched in strength, a tandem can provide the answer. Often it is the only way to cycle together without a compromise on speed. A tandem is subject to greater stresses than an ordinary bicycle so it is well worth investing in a good one. The initial cost may seem considerable, but the advantages are unique as enthusiasts will tell you and the resale value remains high.

Why go touring? Because it combines a feeling of physical exhilaration and freedom with a unique style of exploration. Only on a bike can you travel at human scale speeds and yet cover considerable distances in a day. You can savour the countryside to the full and enjoy the smells and sounds denied to motorised travellers. You can set your own pace, stop where you like, carry your bike over fences and fields or hop on a train if you wish.

Stopping off at small villages you are more likely to be welcomed by locals than the motorist with chicken feathers embossed on his front wheels. You can camp or stay at hotels as you wish. The attraction of camping for the cyclist is that it completes the sense of freedom. Tents made specially for cyclists are available; so are ultra-lightweight cooking utensils. Closed-cell foam sleeping mats weigh very little and so you can equip yourself well at a fraction of the weight you would have had to carry a few years ago. If you would like further information on routes and other aspects of touring in the UK and Europe, two books are recommended:*Adventure Cycling In Europe* by John Rakowski and *The CTC Route Guide* by Christa Gausden and Nicholas Crane.

The success of a tour can be greatly influenced by your choice of basic equipment and by having the necessary tools and spares to cater for mishaps and the unexpected. My first consideration is for comfort *on* the bike rather than *off* it. A small discomfort tolerated around town can become an unbearable pain as a prolonged tour progresses. Also discomfort can come from unexpected places. Contact points such as hands, seat and feet need to be well protected if you intend to do more riding at one time than you are used to doing. "Grab On" foam padding on handlebars will greatly reduce road shock and increase hand comfort. Shorts with chamois or Polartex inserts are much more comfortable than ordinary casual trousers or non-cycling shorts and of course a comfortable, well-adjusted saddle becomes essential. Madison's range of anatomic saddles are accepted by many riders as a great improvement on even the best of the old style leather saddles. Cycling shoes with reinforced soles to spread the pressure of the pedal and facilitate getting in and out of toeclips are also indispensable when touring. Less obvious but equally necessary can be items like peaked caps and sun tan oil. All it takes is one blazing day and an overdose of sun can become dangerously uncomfortable if you are unprepared.

General tips on clothing to bear in mind are that zip-up tops make temperature regulation easy when cycling along. Clothing which doubles on and off the bike means effectively that you need to carry less. Denims however are not recommended for long cycling trips - they are hot and uncomfortable and often restrict movement. The following is a list of items which experience has proved very useful when planning a tour.

Spare spokes
The heavier loads usually carried on a tour may just be enough to cause a broken spoke in an unevenly tensioned wheel. Finding a replacement out in the country is wildly unlikely, so carry a couple of spares remembering that, depending on hub sizes, front and rear spokes may differ in length. You should also take the appropriate removing tool for your freewheel in case a broken spoke occurs on that side of the rear wheel.

Spare inner tubes
An irreparable puncture in mid-Wales is not the same thing as one in your local high street or half a mile from home.

Adjustable spanner
You may like to compromise on weight and exchange your toolkit's selection of small spanners for one larger adjustable. This will cope with most jobs and permit heavier running repairs, like adjusting the headset or removing the freewheel.

Chain rivet extractor
This is essential for chain repair. I have had chain links come apart from time to time. This tool solves the problem in a couple of minutes.

Aztec brake blocks
These blocks, particularly the Aztec Superblock, are highly effective and you may find that you encounter steeper descents than you are used to, with the result that your existing blocks may prove inadequate. Extra loading adds to the problem, so the best brake blocks (well-adjusted and operated with new cables if the old ones are in any way suspect) are really a necessity.

The Blackburn Stopblock
This is an insignificant looking little item but can prove incredibly useful on a heavily-laden bike. It is simply a wedge, stowed on a brake cable when not in use, which fits into the opening of the front brake lever thus putting on the front brake. This prevents the parked bike from rolling and falling when leaned against a wall or post.

Waterbottle
This is not just a flashy racing item. You actually lose a lot of vapour

when cycling and it is wise to replace it on long journeys.

Your own experience may suggest other things you wouldn't like to be without on a tour. As always it's a question of balancing weight against necessity. Any running repairs can leave you with grubby hands. It's quite a good idea to keep a couple of rags tucked under your saddle; use them with a modern hand cleaner like Dirt Squad so that no water is required.

Loading Up

What you take in terms of luggage depends on the length and type of touring you intend. At one extreme you could make do with nothing more than a pair of Pakit Trimline panniers. These versatile aerodynamic panniers can be mounted front or rear and will, if required, hold quite a lot. Then again if you intend to camp, cook and stay on the road for some time, you must consider a more complete set of bags and the most efficient way of carrying heavy loads. There is really no alternative to the system recommended by Jim Blackburn, a Californian engineer whose range of bicycle racks are without question the best in the world. After much research Blackburn recommended the following system as being best: rear panniers held as far forward as heel clearance allows; medium-size front panniers held *low* at the centre of the front wheel; and handlebar bag, if used, to be packed lightly. The critical element of the positioning of the front panniers is that they must be held low to increase stability. To do this Jim Blackburn designed and marketed his Low Rider frame which can be installed without a front carrier and which supports front panniers in this ideal position. There is even a case for using this front position in preference to the more traditional rear one even when small loads are carried. Rigidity is all-important on a heavily loaded bike. Uphill and at speed, a swaying carrier requires extra effort and quite severely affects the handling. All Blackburn carriers are designed with rigidity as a prime requirement whereas many cheaper carriers ignore the problem completely. I've worked through a number of racks over the years and the long trail of rusting, bending and breakages stopped when I bought Blackburn equipment. It is more expensive, but not if you make it your first purchase.

Many pannier systems exist - Carradice and Karrimor are traditional names with well-earned reputations for quality. If you want a complete more versatile system, then I would recommend that you look at the new Pakit range which should satisfy the most demanding tourist.

For many cyclists, touring becomes the ultimate cycling experience. Some become virtual addicts by taking every available opportunity to explore remote landscapes. Thus are born great transcontinental cyclists such as Steve Gill who covers more miles by bike each year than do most motorists. The detailed knowledge of distant lands gained by such cyclists is quite staggering and even if your ambitions are less spectacular, the thrill of completing a tour of any length combines a sense of pleasure with achievement that is quite unique.

Recommended Equipment

Pakit Tents
These tents are ideal for cycle touring. They're very light and compact. The Pakit 1 acommodates one person or two close friends.
Approx. price £100.00.
The Pakit 2 is more spacious with the latest hoop support system.
Approx. price £150.00.

Trangia Cooking Set
Lightweight aluminium pots and stove that nest in each other to save space.
Approx. price £15.00.

Grab-on Handlebar Covering
A thick, shock absorbing foam covering that offers far greater comfort than ordinary tape.
Approx. price £5.50 set.

Madison Super-thin Grips
A thinner and sleeker version of the Grab-on covering.
Approx. price £5.00 set.

Pakit Panniers
A premium quality set of touring bags with loads of clever design features. They're attractively styled in blue with yellow trim and made from quality materials.

FOURNITURES
Maison HERVY
BALANCES
TRANCHEURS
HACHOIRS
SCIES A OS
MATÉRIEL de CUISSON
EXPROPRIATRICE

Recommended Equipment

Jim Blackburn Carriers
Rigid lightweight carriers, suitable for any modern 27″ wheel bicycle. There are a variety of different rear carriers and two front carriers. My favourite combination is the Low Rider front with the SX1 rear carrier.
Approx. price £24.00 each.

Stop Block
Another accessory designed by Jim Blackburn for the tourist. Wedging into the brake lever, this neat device acts as a parking brake, preventing the bike from rolling and toppling over.
Approx. price £3.00.

Books

Adventure Cycling in Europe by John Rakowski
Published by Rodale Press.
Price £8.95.

The C.T.C. Route Guide To Cycling In Britain And Ireland
Published by Oxford Illustrated Press.
Price £7.95.

Cycling in Europe by Nicholas Crane
Published by Oxford Illustrated Press.
Price £7.95.

Addresses

Rough Stuff Fellowship
4 Archway Avenue
Callender
Perthshire FK17 8JZ

Cyclist Touring Club
Cotterell House
69 Meadrow
Godalming
Surrey

League of American Wheelmen
P.O.Box 988
Baltimore
MD 21203
U.S.A.

Federation Francaise de Cyclo-Tourisme
8 Rue Jean-Marie Jego
75013 Paris

Chapter Six

Healthy Returns

Regular cycling and physical fitness.

Cycling and swimming are generally accepted as offering the best all-round exercise there is to be had. The reason is that both activities employ a lot of muscles. It is not only leg muscles which benefit from cycling - arms and stomach muscles are also used, and there is also of course the heart and lung exercise that is the foundation of any fitness programme. I mention swimming also, because, like so many other sporting activities, for me it lacks any real point other than its own completion. Not that there's anything wrong with sport for sport's sake, but cycling has a lot of advantages and getting fit is just one of them. Swimming is of practical use so rarely (liner sinking slowly, lifeboats already put to sea) that it is something that you are not likely to do on a daily basis. The big plus with cycling is that if you incorporate it into your travel routine you get the fitness benefits automatically. I know that if I were to put aside two nights a week to play squash or tennis or to go running, pretty soon I would start finding excuses to put the whole business off until next week. This is the crux of the matter - if you can get into the habit of cycling every day then straight away you have solved the other big fitness problem: *regular* exercise is the only sort that keeps you fit. Sudden bursts of violent activity separated by periods of good intentions will soon guarantee you a horizontal ride in an ambulance.

Perhaps you think you aren't fit enough to abandon bus or train for the bike on a regular basis. If so, cycling offers an unusually easy programme for achieving fitness. The popularity of jogging - a sort of half-hearted running - came about because to run properly you have to be in pretty good condition. Unfit people who were no longer young would quickly do themslves more harm than good. But even jogging can be tiring for someone not used to it, and with the added disadvantages already mentioned, it is understandable why many people begin jogging only to give it up quite quickly. Cycling on the other hand can be undertaken on a very leisurely basis to begin with. You still get to go somewhere, you see things on the way and you have the mild incentive of seeing other cyclists whizz past

you. Gradually you can increase your effort as your ability improves. Even though I can now move at a fair pace on a bike, sometimes I choose to cycle gently and slowly just for the change in pace. There is no minimum level of effort as long as you choose flattish routes to begin with. This is because your body weight is supported; increased effort comes with increased speed or gradient.

For proof of the above you only have to look around you to see cyclists of all ages, in all states of fitness using their bikes for all sorts of different purposes. Sixty and seventy year-olds are less able to turn on the power than youngsters, but you might be surprised at the miles many older cyclists can cover in a day. Many an eager young cycle tourist has sped past elderly riders early in the day only to be overtaken by them hours later, still going at a steady untiring pace. This in fact is the secret for any cyclist - finding your pace and sticking to it means that you never get tired and can cover surprisingly long distances comfortably. Your food requirements will depend on your metabolism, but lack of nourishment will quickly result in a sensation of lethargic weakness which may discourage you into thinking that you are physically incapable of cycling strongly.

This question of confidence in your own ability is particularly important in relation to fitness because it is so easy to do it all wrong and form the mistaken impression that you are simply not fit enough for regular cycling exercise. If you are a novice, the single most important breakthrough is overcoming the barrier of inability. Say you live fifteen miles from your place of work - that's a thirty mile round trip. By bike? Every day? Am I joking? Not at all, in fact many cyclists (as I've already indicated) secretly wish that they lived further from their job in order to boost their ride. If you're sceptical try a trip of an equivalent length one weekend, taking it easy. Time yourself. Build up your ability. Soon you will have broken that barrier. All that's required is a good bike and a sensible programme of improvement. The final step is to incorporate your cycling into your routine - if not commuting, then some regular weekly appointments or trips. The benefits are enormous. If you play some sport you will find that the "background" fitness gained from regular cycling is invaluable. Whilst every activity makes its own specific requirements on muscles and co-ordination, the stamina you build up from heart and lung (aerobic) exercise when cycling will give you a flying start whatever you do - tennis, football, squash, running up stairs .... .

A few tips which are fundamental to all good cycling are perhaps worth mentioning here, since bad habits might prove discouraging to the novice keen to get fit. Get your saddle adjusted to the correct height. Almost everyone's natural inclination is to ride with the saddle too low. This gives a false feeling of security, causes the rider to bend his legs too much, robs him of pedalling power and can impair posture causing further discomfort. Position one pedal at its lowest point where the crank is in line with the seat tube. Adjust the saddle so that when you are sitting on it you can rest your heel on the pedal whilst keeping your leg straight. This arrangement permits a slight bend at the knee when the ball of the foot rests on the pedal. Experiment with the angle of the saddle, sliding it backwards and forwards and tilting it up and down for the most comfortable angle. Keep changing it until you get it right.

Don't confuse immense effort with getting fit. So don't push big gears - the technique is to turn the pedals as fast as you can conveniently manage and select the correct gear to arrive at your road speed. A helpful analogy is that of a car engine: if you imagine trying to pull away in third gear then you simply place an absurd amount of strain on the engine. Far better to rev high and engage a low gear. In fact the principle of pedalling is similar to that of a rotating crankshaft: the rider's job is to turn the cranks as if each were a handle (toe-straps and shoe cleats both aid in rotating rather than simply stabbing at the pedals) and to translate this consistent power into different road speeds by means of the gears.

Even if you are uncompetitive by nature, you're likely to find that the challenge posed by an overtaking cyclist is often hard to resist. For some people it is then just a short step to competitive cycling. Long and punishing hours of training await those who aim for the top in the field. The distances logged daily by leading professionals require an astonishing degree of dedication and single mindedness of purpose, stern preparation for what is often a gruelling sport. The pain and exhaustion one sees etched in the faces of the competitors in races like Paris-Roubaix and the Tour de France are evidence of what it costs to reach the top. Few sports demand such extended periods of courage and determination, but there are of course great numbers of cyclists who derive immense satisfaction and enjoyment from competitive cycling without taking things to this extreme.

Computer technology has come to cycling like everything else. Modern measuring devices are computerised and a host of information about your cycling performance is available in digital readout at the touch of a button. It's true that the first trip I made in the company of one of these computers got off to a hazy start, since the instruction booklet looked ominously thick and the advertised features sounded so sophisticated that the computer looked quite frightening sitting there on the handlebar. After a while though it proved indispensable, offering a wide range of information about my cycling performance (or lack of it) and generally proving to be a very useful little gadget.

Modern home trainers convert your bike into an exercise machine that requires no balancing and can be adjusted to simulate road conditions. Electronic devices are available to monitor pulse rate, measure equivalent distance travelled and so on, enabling you to maintain a regular fitness programme. I have read of an instance where an "indoor cyclist", tracing his progress on an atlas, circumnavigated the world in the comfort of his own living room, listening to headphone music and reading a book.

In fact the title of this chapter reflects my own feelings on the matter of fitness - I am most happy with it when it is achieved incidentally. The dogged pursuit of fitness for its own sake has inspired and sustained many people, but I am not one of them. I am pleased to feel strong and healthy, but I am more pleased that it has been achieved as a by-product of something which is always enjoyable and frequently practical.

Recommended Equipment

Styrene Toe Clips
Made from a black nylon which seems virtually unbreakable, these light clips hold their shape well. A good modern innovation!
Approx. price £3.00 pair.

Avocet Cyclometer
This is the best of the new generation of electronic gadgets for cyclists that I've come across. It's accurate and easy to fit and use, and it's small and unobtrusive - which I think is important.
Approx. price £25.00.

Cateye Solar Cyclist Computer
Powered by solar energy, this compact unit has so many functions, you could never possibly be bored on your bike.
Approx. price £50.00.

Tunturi Pulsemeter
From the well known makers of exercise machines, this device clips onto an ear lobe and monitors changes in your pulse rate.
Approx. price £66.00.

Elite Cycle Turbo Trainer
A machine that instantly converts your bicycle into a stationery home exerciser. A good space saver.
Approx. price £56.00.

Chapter Seven

Silent Running

Upgrading the basic machine.

I once took a motorcycle engine completely to pieces. There were hundreds of bits, all of which had to be removed to get at the final broken one. Disassembled it looked like a nightmare. My education had done little to prepare me for life's practical tasks and only natural curiosity had made me gradually more competent at fixing things and finding out how they worked. This was the big one. Eventually I put all the bits together again and bolted the engine back on the frame. I connected all the leads and hoses, switched on the engine and pushed down the kickstart. It fired first time and ran beautifully. I recounted this little success story to a friend who said, "Of course, when you've put it together right it *has* to work - it can't do anything else." Of course he was right - I was still being superstitious, still feeling that machines have got it in for human beings, still feeling that there is an element of luck involved. There isn't, and if you are one of those people who shy away from practical tasks, your bike is the ideal place to educate yourself. Your bike is in a sense an extension of your body, it translates your effort into rolling motion and for this reason you will quickly sense when it isn't working well. Conversely, the efficient, responsive feel of a newly overhauled machine is a delight when you've been persevering with the sloppy feel of ill-adjusted components for any length of time. The bearings, levers, chains and sprockets of a bicycle are all accessible and, with the bike on a stand, can be seen in operation. The principles involved are simple and are basic to any number of other mechanical inventions. Anyone can learn to maintain a bicycle to some degree at least, and there is great satisfaction in repairing or maintaining your own machine, even if you don't consider yourself to be mechanically minded.

I am mainly interested in motivating you to maintain your bike because that is part of the cycling experience. Start by getting a simple grasp of what a bike has to do. See how the design problems have been solved. For example, discover for yourself which parts are subject to the greatest wear. Tyres seem obvious of course, and the rear one more so than the front. Why? Because it suffers not only when you brake (as does the front one) but also when you accelerate. Does this simple conclusion suggest any course of action? What about swapping over the tyres when the discrepancy becomes noticeable? OK, you may say, that's simple and obvious. But continue the exercise. Why does your chain skip occasionally but not all the time? Can it be a faulty link or doesn't it happen regularly enough? Maybe one sprocket on your freewheel is worn more than the others. Check and see every time it happens - are you always on that sprocket? If so, that's it. When you turn your bike upside down and rest it on handlebars and seat you may notice that the wheels don't always rotate freely. Why is this? - they turn OK when it's the right way up. Maybe the brake cables are distorted. This results in a gentle application of the brake. No problem, but remember the principle for the day your saddlebag comes adrift and presses on the rear brake cable and causes the brake blocks to bind on the wheel. Training yourself to think like this prepares you not only for more sophisticated bicycle adjustments, but also for a whole host of other practical problems.

A sensible idea is to buy yourself a workstand. This will hold your bike firmly and so avoid that moment when, as you perform some delicate adjustment, the bike starts rolling away from you, denting and gouging as it goes. It will also allow you to turn the pedals and watch the brakes and gears in operation while standing in a relaxing position. Proper tools are essential if you wish to have the satisfaction of doing any job efficiently. Seek professional advice if you don't know what you will need.

My intention is to outline an approach to some of the jobs you will have to perform if your bike is going to continue to run sweetly. Of course you may have to seek more detailed instructions elsewhere - a suggested list of authoritative sources appears at the end of the chapter - but I hope to indicate what to look out for and to offer a few useful hints.

There is no point in being unduly nervous about maintenance, although it is best not to start an unfamiliar task if you are going to need the bike in half an hour's time. Most of the mechanics of a bike are obviously exposed and accessible and the best way to learn about them is by tackling the tasks straight off, learning as you go. Caution is needed but not trepidation.

Wheels

Wheels should be checked regularly to ensure that they are running true. A poorly-tensioned wheel can easily lose its shape and this results in broken spokes. Beyond a certain point it will rapidly deteriorate towards a state of unreliability or even collapse. One eighth of an inch sideways travel is an acceptable amount of distortion, but more than that means trouble. If you don't feel competent to put the matter right with judicious use of a spoke key, then have it seen to by your local repairer. Depending on the severity of use, wheels might have to be checked as often as every two months, although the problem is minimised if a reputable wheel builder makes your wheels in the first place taking into account the sort of use you will be giving them. Knowing your requirements for speed and reliability plus the kind of surfaces you are likely to encounter will allow a wheelbuilder to recommend what type of hubs, spokes and rims you should have and how much they will cost. In my experience hand-built wheels are a good investment.

Chain, front chainwheels and rear sprockets

The chain, front chainwheels and rear sprockets are transmission components which are all too often neglected. In common with any mechanical parts subjected to friction, they will wear out. How quickly depends on what you do to them, or more usually what you don't do to them. The chain in particular is subjected to severe stresses and constant wear and deserves a little attention. You should keep it clean and lightly lubricated. I have always found LPS3 aerosol a convenient lubricant but there are a number of other brands that will do an adequate job. Avoid lubricants which wash off at the first drop of rain. This said, cleaning a chain is a potentially messy business - the amalgam of dirt and lubricant that transfers itself to your hands, clothes, pets, children, doorhandles and wallpaper can be tricky to remove, so you had best approach the task with plenty of rags and maybe rubber gloves. The use of a "Superlink" connecting link makes chain removal much easier since you don't have to use a rivet extractor and complete removal of the chain makes it easier to clean and gives better access to the rear derailleur and rear sprockets. You should replace your chain every two thousand miles. It will last longer, but due to stretching it will be wearing sprockets and chainwheels as it distorts. This is bad economy since chains are not as expensive as either of these components.

Bearings
There are only seven sets of bearings on a bicycle. They comprise those in the pedals, hubs, freewheel, headset and bottom bracket. Naturally these should be adequately lubricated from time to time and, just as importantly, accurately adjusted. To achieve this, it is necessary to possess the proper tools for working on all the bearing parts. These should be available from your dealer or by mail order from Freewheel. Having taken the trouble to clean the bearings it is worth using a good lubricant like Red 'S' waterproof grease which is an ideal bearing grease.

Brakes
To neglect brake maintenance is more than unwise - it is potentially dangerous. It's not unknown for a brake block to part company with its shoe or for a brake cable to snap where it enters the lever. New bikes are particularly prone to these and other mishaps if you don't check them over. In early use the vibration can make things work loose that may initially have seemed quite well tightened. A few moments and a few simple tools are all that are required. Particularly useful for brake adjustment is a device known as a third-hand tool which presses the calipers to the rim leaving both hands free to take up the slack in the cable. Any doubts about the soundness of a cable should result in your replacing it. A good choice is the "Aztec" brand of self-lubricating cables, but these and all others stretch a little when new, so be prepared for fairly early readjustment after fitting them.

Tyres
Tyres form the vital link between you and the road, so treat them properly. Regular inspections can reveal that a blow-out is imminent or that a piece of glass is embedded and well on its way towards the inner tube. Recommended tyre pressures should be maintained because that's how the tyre was designed to be used. The correct pressure will help tyres to survive potholes and other road hazards. Tyres like those in the Nutrak range are designed to run on slightly higher-than-average pressures. Combined with the right tread design, this factor also reduces the rolling resistance to provide increased pedalling efficiency. I always choose skinwall tyres which, although more expensive due to their rather complex construction, are fast and durable and capable of holding higher pressures despite their lighter and thinner casings. This raises the question of how to achieve these pressures without having a heart attack. 100 lb per square inch

can cause an orange mist to drift in front of your eyes if you try to achieve it with a flimsy hand pump. Keeping a workshop plunger type pump at home will make the job a lot easier. The most efficient type of hand pumps however, are those with push-on connectors, not hose connectors. The "Truflo" brand is probably the best on the market, particularly the "Airloc" model.

Gears

Gear adjustment is a critical matter and must not be taken for granted, especially if accidental misalignment occurs, for example when your bike falls over. I have seen experienced cyclists change gear onto the biggest rear sprocket - and beyond, into the spokes. When you reach this stage, the best plan is to fling the bike down and shout at it. Better by far to periodically check both front and rear gear mechanisms for precisely the right amount of travel. A small screwdriver is all that is required. If gears keep changing themselves, then the likely cause is insufficient tension on the friction clamp of the gear lever. Simply tightening the screw at the centre of the lever barrel should do the trick. Overtightening will make the action too stiff to operate the lever easily.

To successfully complete any of the above tasks, all you need is the right tools and a positive approach. You will certainly find out things on the way - maybe things peculiar to your bike, maybe fundamental mechanical principles you had never really thought about before. In the end you will find that working on your bicycle to keep it in good running order can prove to be a satisfying and rewarding part of the cycling experience.

Recommended Equipment

Leda Workstand
Having the bicycle held securely with the moving parts operational is a great aid to maintenance work.
Approx. price £27.00.

Super Link
This item may appear gimmicky at first but in fact it's very useful for easily removing and refitting your chain.
Approx. price £3.50.

Red S Waterproof Grease
Besides the favourable qualities of the grease, the tube it comes in provides an excellent dispensing nozzle.
Approx. price 65p.

Truflo Airloc Pump
Tyre inflation is quicker and simpler with one of these pumps.
Approx. price £6.00.

Aztec Replacement Cable Kit
Like everything else, there are different qualities of cables, and these are the very best.

LPS 3 Lubricant
The aerosal application is very convenient and this is a good chain lubricant. It is suitable for the chain and most moving parts on a bicycle that require regular attention.
Approx. price £2.50.

The Penguin Bicycle Handbook by Rob van der Plas
Published by Penguin Books.
Price £3.95.

85T

Chapter Eight

Moving On

Satisfaction from fine-tuning the bike.

There is nothing wrong with feeling dissatisfied with the bike that seemed fine when you bought it and is still working reasonably well. The reason is probably that you have improved as a rider and have come to expect more from your machine. This is bound to happen to people who buy bikes that are only just about good enough for their imagined requirement; it's understandable too. The problem facing novices is that they find it difficult to anticipate the steady process of improvement that all cyclists experience and so cannot easily imagine the appetite for a better machine that usually accompanies it. So how do cyclists improve? They improve not just in fitness but in all sorts of ways which are not always obvious. Regardless of your level of fitness, you learn to pace yourself so that you arrive at your destination exhilarated rather than wheezing incomprehensibly. You start gently, build up the pedalling power and learn to monitor your body's resources so that you know when to slacken off or step up your effort. It sounds like common sense but many inexperienced riders see a longish ride as a challenge, set off with all the power they can muster and run out of steam very quickly. Once moving you can make your journey smoother by making skillful use of the gears. Often I see riders setting off from traffic lights in an absurdly high gear left over from an earlier downhill run. Anticipation is what it is all about, and an intelligent reading of the situation ahead will place you in the correct gear for moving off from a standstill, and eliminate unnecessary extra effort. The same approach will lead you to use your brakes less often - constant clutching at the brake levers is often more of a nervous habit than the result of any genuine need to stop or slow down. Correct positioning on the road and a trained eye for escape routes and likely developments all around you will enable you to leave the brakes alone and maintain your momentum in situations where you don't *have* to stop.

The question of cadence - the rate at which you turn the cranks - is one about which purists argue interminably. Even before I ever learned about the notion, I had got into the habit of pedalling quite fast and so I tend to support the view that most people's cadence is too slow. Of course the rate of pedalling is directly related to gearing and once you have sorted out your preferred range of gears, I suggest you select a lower gear and pedal a little faster than your usual rate. Clean and accurate gear-shifts will allow you to turn that momentum into fluent road speed with less risk of strained muscles and early fatigue.

Hill-climbing - the big horror for novices - becomes for the experienced cyclist a simple matter of choosing the best technique. Equipped with the appropriate gears you can attack the hill aggressively at the bottom - often the sheer momentum will take out most of the effort which drains the plodder. Alternatively, you may choose the method which I prefer, that is to select a low gear and find a fast pedalling rate which you can maintain easily and just keep going. Either way you will discover that timing and accuracy of gear-changing is crucial. A misjudged change half-way up a steep gradient will rob you of momentum or rhythm making the task difficult and disheartening.

You will find other little tricks and techniques for yourself and the eventual result will be that your whole attitude towards your bike gradually shifts. Compared to the superhuman cycling achievements of some people, my own are modest, but I would consider an evening cycle ride to visit friends (say a twenty-five mile round trip) as quite normal. There is no sense of "a trip", it is simply a natural way to travel once you have improved sufficiently to consider your bike as a natural extension of yourself.

As you become more experienced as a cyclist, it will gradually become more clear to you that ordinary clothing is not entirely suited to cycling. Shoes get marked and worn, shirts and jeans tend to part leaving you with a cold back, trousers get baggy around the knees. You may at first feel understandably reluctant to look like a fully-fledged club cyclist, but their's is the best equipment and how far you want to adopt it depends on how serious you get about cycling. I still cycle in jeans and tee shirts some of the time, but they are no substitute for the comfort of purpose-made cycling clothing which quite literally makes me feel more purposeful and energetic. Shoes and trousers are the most important items. The choice in footwear used to be limited to either old-style leather-soled touring or racing shoes, which made walking seem like a new skill to be learned all over again, or ordinary shoes which offered no resistance to pedal pressure and quickly showed signs of toe-clip abrasion. These days modern touring shoes are quite different and I have cycled thousands of miles in a pair of Madison shoes and walked a few hundred city miles as well. Styled as trainers, but complete with pedal-pressure reinforcement, these are virtually indestructible and incredibly comfortable. For those unconvinced of the need for specialist clothing and accessories, these shoes are a good place to start. Depending on your enthusiasm you may then want to consider shorts. Here again, Madison offer the ones I prefer - stretch-fabric touring style shorts which I find more practical than the traditional close-fitting black ones. In winter I wear tights or long cycling trousers designed with high backs to eliminate the freezing gap which generally appears between the upper and lower half of conventional clothing when you are crouched over the handlebar. For fast training or racing there is no substitute for the traditional close-fitting garments favoured by serious racing cyclists. There are various continental manufacturers of such clothing and quality can vary. One of the best and most reliable makes is Castelli, recognisable by the distinctive Scorpion trade mark.

Browsing in your favourite cycle shop can be very pleasant once you have sampled a few purpose-made items of clothing and know what to look for, but if this is not practical or possible where you live, then you should acquire the Freewheel catalogue, published annually and now the definitive guide for all cycling goods.

Recommended Equipment

Madison Cyclists' Touring Shoes
A quality leather shoe with a specially reinforced sole that I have found both hardwearing and comfortable.
Approx. price £28.00.

Madison Cyclists' Touring Shorts
Ordinary shorts can be very uncomfortable to cycle any distance in. These are made from a stretch fabric with a special inner seat lining and are a far better solution for cycling.
Approx. price £17.00.

Castelli Racing Shorts
Developed over many years, this type of short is the best thing for serious cycling. Castelli is the premier name in competition cycle clothing.
Approx. price £16.00.

Freewheel Cyclists' Equipment Guide
£1.00 from major newsagents or direct from Freewheel, 275 West End Lane, London NW6.

REVELL

Chapter Nine

Basic Improvements

Mastering the skills.

The bicycle is a brilliantly unique invention. It's nearest relative, the motorcycle, feels remarkably different even if you just roll the thing gently downhill. In fact the similarities are superficial. At heart the bicycle is a dynamic machine in which pre-loaded elastic structures (the wheels) support a rigid, yet resilient, frame which quite literally becomes an extension of the rider's physique. This notion of natural extension is the key one. You combine yourself with a good bicycle to convert your energy into fluid motion. On a motorcycle you merely sit and learn to control its independent power. It is then easy to see how the uninformed cyclist, sitting bolt upright on his leaden machine and forcing round the cranks with alternate jabs completely misses that sense of harmony between man and bicycle that can be so finely developed between modern machine and modern rider. In order to experience this unique thrill of cycling it helps to understand exactly which components combine to deliver the response. And as your skills and familiarity with your cycle increase, there will inevitably come a time when you begin to feel this or that limitation. It may be something obvious like an inadequate saddle that first makes itself felt. Let's consider that example for a moment. If you have bought a moderately-priced bike, it may be that the saddle is OK only for short rides but becomes painful if you spend any length of time on it. Nowadays the pre-formed anatomic saddle with leather covering has replaced the traditional hide saddle as the cure for saddle discomfort. The Madison range has its imitators but just because a saddle looks anatomical - that is, with raised pads and a central groove - it doesn't necessarily mean it will be your anatomy it will be sympathetic to; the quality of the materials and the care taken in design are what determine the comfort.

The saddle then is a relatively inexpensive component which can also be transferred from one bike to another if desired. When it comes to other components, get to know what you're doing before committing yourself to an illogical improvement. Installing an expensive replacement component on a fairly inexpensive bike will not significantly increase that bike's resale value. In addition you may find that the anticipated enjoyment of that new component is compromised by other inadequacies which only make themselves felt later. You should therefore make sure you understand the relative importance of the various parts of your bike so that you can upgrade it in an informed way.

The fundamental truth is that, more than anything else, it is the frame and wheels which determine how a bike feels. Changing either of these is more likely to have a noticeable effect than changing all of the remaining components. This said you can of course upgrade your machine bit by bit to good effect and the bottom bracket is perhaps the next item to consider for improvement.

A common technique for improvement is to buy a new, better quality frame, transfer your existing components and then gradually replace them one at a time. Conversely, you may dress up your old frame with new components, renewing the frame last of all. Either way you need to know as much about frames as possible. If you are an inexperienced cyclist the best way to appreciate a good frame is to borrow a good bike if you can. A handmade frame with lightweight tubing feels very lively and when you have become accustomed to this feeling you should be able to appreciate minor changes of frame geometry as well. This is usually identified by the angle made by the seat tube to the cross tube. More often than not the seat tube is parallel to the head tube. Thus one calls a frame for example 73 degrees parallel. This is as it happens, the most common basis for a modern fast touring frame. 72 degree frames with a longer wheel base are more suitable for heavily laden, long distance touring. 74 degree frames with a shorter wheelbase are much more reponsive and designed for road racing. Another important aspect of frame geometry that affects a bike's response is the fork trail which is governed by a combination of the head tube angle and the rake in the fork themselves. When buying a frame from a prestige builder you can usually rely on them to design the frame geometry sensibly. Production model cycles on the other hand can be more whimsically designed and one should assume nothing.

If you are buying a frame you should be aware that handmade frames are no longer the exclusive province of the custom made market. Standard design, handmade frames are available off the shelf at reasonable prices. Make sure you get a good one - I can

Red S Unicell Bottom Bracket
Besides the enclosed sealed bearing cartridge, I like the feature that allows fine side to side adjustment.
Approx. price £22.00.

Aztec Superblocks
If you're replacing worn brake blocks or seeking better braking, these are the ones to go for. There is also a version which fits cantilever brakes.
Approx. price £3.50 pair.

Miche Pedals
A serviceable copy of the famous Campagnolo pedals, these pedals are a good cheaper alternative.
Approx. price £11.00.

Chapter Ten

Splashing Out

High performance cycling with the top equipment.

Often the path to a really first-class bike is a long and cautious one. Few people lured by the idea of a good bike are prepared to spend six hundred pounds or so first time round - you have to be a convert to start thinking in these terms. Let's assume that you have made the decision to get the best; even if you don't actually do it, there are lessons to be learned by considering how to arrive at a no-expense-spared machine. Expenditure alone will guarantee nothing except perhaps a brisk note from your bank manager. Neither is there a recipe for the ultimate - manufacturers are constantly updating their ranges and last year's best may not be this year's best. Whatever the superficial variations though, the underlying approach does not change: the heart of any bike is the frame.

If we restrict the exercise to either touring or racing requirements, we can examine the best way to go about getting what you want. In each case a custom-built frame is what you should look for. If you need a touring frame, many dealers and builders offer a custom service; someone with a proven reputation or a good recommendation is clearly what to aim for, otherwise you have to assess quality from what is on display or from the degree of professionalism shown by the people in question. You should then be able to assume that the basic geometry and size will be taken care of, and so you can dwell on details like what brazed-on extras you require, including mountings for cantilever brakes if that is your fancy. More or less any specified brazing can be incorporated allowing the tourist to attach his favourite bits and pieces in the neatest and most secure manner.

When selecting components, it is important to work in logical groups - carrier and panniers; transmission components; hubs, spokes and rims for the wheel. The tourist is also well advised to balance his choice of components with considerations of spares availability in other countries. The ultimate touring chainset should be able to incorporate a wide spread of chainrings and a sealed

bearing bottom bracket is a sensible idea. The Red 'S' Unicell bottom bracket is a good choice and will give smooth running for many thousands of miles. Many makes of chain are available but Promex L, Regina CX and Sedisport are among the best. Whatever chain you choose should incorporate a Superlink for easy chain removal: this obviates the need for carrying a rivet extractor with you and so, indirectly, results in weight-saving. The rear derailleur might be a Huret Duopar, Campagnolo Rally or Shimano RD, and the front changer a Huret Success or Shimano FD. Ratchet levers, with their distinctive 'clicking' sound, are better than the cheaper models that rely on friction alone. (Consider specifying brazed-on lever fittings when ordering your frame). When it comes to brakes, Campagnolo is the name again, although as mentioned earlier, yours is the option to provide for cantilever brakes which are a very positive method of stopping a heavily loaded touring cycle.

A top-class wheelbuilder is *de rigeur* for your dream bike and besides the individual components, you can also specify a particular spoking pattern.

Tyres are a matter of preference, and tyres from the Nutrak range are among the best. Worth considering are the Extra, which is a 27 x 1⅜ tyre designed to withstand the side-wall stress which can result from a heavy touring load, and the Marathon which has a skinwall construction and is also available in 700x32c.

Pedals for touring are often similar to racing designs unless you have a preference for platform-type pedals which spread the pressure slightly more than the quill type. Here price will usually reflect quality.

Headsets to consider are Campagnolo Record Road and Red 'S', but make sure you get something of quality. This component is often underestimated and can noticeably affect the feel of your machine; whilst the ship may not exactly be spoiled by this ha'porth of tar, it may be adversely affected if care is not taken in choosing and installing something good.

I have dwelt on touring because I imagine that is what most people aspire to, whether it is to actually tour or rather to commute and joy-ride on the very best. If what you want is a top-class racing bike, you probably already have quite a thorough knowledge of what you aspire to. The question of the custom frame becomes more critical and your framebuilder will probably want to take into consideration your present machine and your specific requirements as to geometry and handling characteristics. Your choice of components may well be determined by going for groups, and as likely as not these will turn out to be made by Campagnolo, who it must be said, have the history of quality to justify their somewhat rarified prices. Campagnolo's 50th Anniversary set would grace any machine. Other famous brands are Cinelli for handlebars and stems, and Clement for tubular tyres.

At the end of this chapter are two specification tables which indicate how your ultimate bike might be arrived at. There is no reason why you should not arrive at a different superbike, but you will have arrived at it by similar methods to those I have suggested in this chapter: by thinking logically about related areas of your bike, bearing in mind that one poor component can reduce your enjoyment of other excellent ones.

My more general feeling about splashing out has less to do with one big spending spree than with the mental attitude which accompanies it. To spend a thousand pounds on a bike appears ridiculous to many people, but it is only a question of how you look at it, since a thousand pounds will buy you superb engineering and a beautiful machine. Many people are pleased to spend as *little* as one thousand pounds on a second-hand car which will entitle them to pay even more in tax, insurance, service and repair bills whilst they avoid exercise, pollute the atmosphere and stand a chance of adding to the number of people killed on the road. When this bargain finally falls in a heap of rust two or three years later, the owner will often say how good it was and how he has no cause for complaint. We each have our own way of valuing things but to me the one thousand pound bike is much better value - what other consumer durable is going to last for twenty years or more?

Most of the supposed advantages of the car in the end come down to the fact that a society conditioned to depend on cars will always be less sympathetic to any form of transport which hasn't got four wheels, an internal combustion engine and a steering wheel at the front. This state of affairs will change so slowly as to be of no immediate relevance to you and me today - not that this should give rise to complacency - but I dwell on it simply to reassert my original point: looked at in anything but the most biased terms, bikes are great value, even expensive bikes.

'Splashing Out' on a Touring Bike - a suggested specification

Frame: Made to measure from Reynolds 531 ST tubing with: two sets of bottle cage bosses; brazed on bosses for cantilever brakes; Jim Blackburn rear carrier and front Low Rider; mounting plate and concealed tubing for Byka lamps and generator; vertical forged dropouts.
Wheels: Maxicar quick release hubs, Super Champion model 58 rims, Madison single butted stainless steel spokes, 40 spoked rear wheel laced four cross, 36 spoked front wheel laced three cross.
Chainset: Red S 99 triple chainset, 170mm crank arm length, 48, 40, 28 chainrings.
Bottom Bracket: Red S Unicell sealed unit.
Handlebars: SR Alloy Randonneur.
Stem: SR Foursir Aero.
Gears: Huret Duopar rear, Huret Success front with Huret brazed on levers.
Pedals: Campagnolo Strada XL, with 'Proclips' and Binda Extra Straps.
Brakes: Shimano De Ore Cantilever with Aztec Superblocks.
Chain: Regina CX.
Tyres: Nutrak Marathon Beltguard with Nutrak tubes.
Freewheel: Shimano nickle plated extra duty 13-15-17-24-28-32.
Headset: Red S.
Saddle: Madison G12.
Seat Pin: Campagnolo Super Record.
Carriers: Jim Blackburn SX1 rear, Low Rider front.
Extras: Mirrycle mirror, Grab-on handlebar covers, Byka Electronic Light System, Truflo Airloc pump, Duroplast mudguards.
Total Price: Approx. £850.00.

My Ideal Racing Cycle

Frame: Made to measure from Reynolds 753 tubing with Campagnolo Super Record forged ends.
Components: Campagnolo Super Record Group set, including Campagnolo Freewheel.
Wheels: Campagnolo hubs, Ascenti Super Strada hardalloy rims, Madison double butted stainless spokes, built three cross front and rear with 28 spokes front and 32 rear.
Tyres: Clement Criteriums.
Saddle: Madison Pro Am.
Handlebar: Cinelli model 66, 42cms.
Stem: Cinelli Record,
Total Price: Approx. £1300.00.

Chapter Eleven

Wheeling and Dealing

The bike shop revolution.

The history of cycling in the UK is, for better and worse, to be gauged in those places that all cyclists must visit from time to time: the bike shops. I suppose any leisure activity is served by retail outlets which reflect its character, but not so long ago the bike trade spawned a breathtaking variety of shops. At one end was the crazy old museum full of bits and pieces the purpose of which even the proprietor had forgotten. At the other end was the modern well-equipped shop tuned in to the real reason why people were flocking back to cycling. In between were all sorts of places. Depending on your requirement any of them might just turn out to have had what you wanted; in some shops the odds were definitely against it.

When as an adult I first became interested in cycling I dutifully presented myself at the premises of an "established" cycle shop for advice, for a bike and for some accessories - then strange things occurred. As soon as I went in there was a sensation of stepping back in time. When the hands of the clock had stopped whizzing backwards to about 1949 an elderly man eating a sandwich stepped out of the shadows and listened to my requirements with a world-weary air. Clearly I had come at an inconvenient moment i.e. when he was open. In the end he handed me over to a youth who had joined him from the gloom and to whom I had to repeat everything I'd already said. Judging by his frown the weight of this information sat heavily on the lad's shoulders. He decided to go back and look for the original man who subsequently reappeared, his sandwich only slightly smaller. After half an hour we had established that what I wanted was not on display. There was a remote chance that something similar existed in the store room. The store room might have been on Mars for all the keenness they showed to go and look. After some squabbling between themselves they both went and I took the opportunity to leave.

I am told that the experience was exceptionally bad, but to a lesser degree those attitudes used to exist in a bike trade which had little confidence in itself and its own future. With hindsight it is easy to see the opportunities which those traditional shops so frequently missed. The shop I went to next and which eventually became my favourite was, by contrast, ahead of its time. The first difference I noticed was that the staff were outnumbered by the customers. There was also a noticeable keenness to do business. The stock was new. This was another world and there were quite a few telling encounters in that shop in those early days of the bicycle boom. Elderly customers more familiar with the other type of shop would turn up to buy some trivial component expecting three-quarters of an hour of head scratching and sighing. To be given what they'd asked for in fifteen seconds left them feeling vaguely cheated and anxious to prolong the proceedings. Thus an incompetent trade had conditioned a customer to match. And there would be casual converts to cycling, still convinced that no bike could conceivably cost more than five pounds. These customers would pick up a handful of small components in the manner of someone choosing an assortment of sweets from Woolworths only to drop them as if red hot upon being told the price. More disappointed still were those who dragged in grotesquely deformed bicycles - machines with corroded bearings, immovable cables, elliptical wheels and rigid chains - demanding that they be made roadworthy at nominal cost.

Soon all this began to change. The turnabout came as an indirect result of the expanding US bicycle market. Relatively free from the traditional caution of the British bike business, American cyclists began to demand the sort of hi-tech equipment which could be quite easily produced as long as there was a market for it. High quality Japanese products began to appear and others followed. It became possible to buy and equip first rate machines in the US. Those same manufacturers were more than pleased to supply other markets and so a new breed of retailers suddenly became successful in the UK. As likely as not they were young and able to see the bicycle and its possibilities for what it really was - a brilliant and timeless invention ripe for refinement for a whole new generation of consumers. These consumers were better educated about health and pollution as well as being accustomed to appreciating well made machines and design out of function.

While all this was going on one section of the old UK bicycle heirarchy was carrying on much as before, with steady success. The frame builders kept supplying their customers with top quality frames which had and continue to have a worldwide

reputation for quality. Perhaps the economics of frame building were more favourable, perhaps the appeal of the craftsman outlasts all but the most biting recession - in any case the British framebuilder survived and his product is stilll eagerly sought.

The other area in which Britain retained its cycling reputation was as a touring nation. Simply because Britain is good touring country it has traditionally produced good touring bikes and accessories. Nowadays, with these two areas of supremacy largely unscathed, Britain's bicycle trade has hauled itself up by the bootlaces and now outstrips the rest of Eurpoe in attitude and approach to cycling goods for the non-competitive cyclist. In the racing world of course it is Italy and France that are in the vanguard, but there are signs that in the broader cycling spectrum too Europe is ready to follow the lead of the UK just as the UK picked up on the American revival.

This leaves Britain today with an ever-improving cycle business. The trade shows reflect vigorous growth and a gradual falling by the wayside of the old hidebound attitudes. Taiwan is energetically seeking to follow in the footsteps of Japan and one suspects that it is not just cheap labour that makes such countries strive towards the production of bicycles and accessories far beyond the expectations of the indigenous cycling population. Back home at street level you will have more difficulty finding the old-style shops, but beware too of those eager to ride on the back of the bicycle boom but unable or unwilling to back up sales with good advice born of enthusiasm. And as mentioned earlier beware too of the department store or warehouse dealer for whom bikes are no more than units to be sold and never seen again. A badly assembled washing machine may turn out to be an inconvenience but a badly adjusted or shoddy bike may be dangerous.

If you are new to cycling it's as well to bear in mind that a little background research will stand you in good stead when visiting the bike shop of your choice. This book will hopefully have put cycling today into some sort of context and monthly cycling publications will give you valuable updated information on prices and availability as well as a wealth of other cycling information. "Bicycle" magazine currently reflects most accurately the new spirit of cycling whilst one or two others deal with more specific areas of cycling interest such as racing or BMX.

Finally don't be put off the quaint old cycle shop once you

have got it in perspective. As long as you don't believe that it reflects the true face of cycling, there is enormous enjoyment to be had from the kind of bicycle Aladdin's cave which still seems to exist in some places. More than once an unexpected snag in some strange town has forced me to plunge back into the time-warp of some old bike shop where the simplest request is received as though you have asked for the Holy Grail and a long search is undertaken by the proprietor who patiently sifts through large wooden drawers as often as not marked "rice" or "tapioca". When at last with a broad smile he withdraws something from a murky recess it turns out to be a quite different part that he had been unable to find for some previous long-departed customer and which he seems to find all the more welcome because of its unexpectedness. The sure way to identify a shop like this is from its window display. The goods on show will always contain two things: a dusty and discoloured bicycle lamp which accepts only batteries of the type that became unavailable ten years before; and a miniature fan-shaped display of replacement valve rubbers. Behind these tell-tale exhibits will be a sun-bleached poster showing a now defunct brand of bicycle being ridden by a girl looking like Mary Pickford. Sooner or later you will find such a shop but if you happen to need a computerised speedometer be prepared for disappointment.

Conclusion

Other Directions

Bikes are only just beginning! The technological revolution which has released all those refinements already discussed in relation to bicycle design also suggests other ways that human-powered vehicles might be developed. At cycle shows and other places where enthusiasts meet you can now see a variety of Human Powered Vehicles (HPVs) being tried out by their owners or inventors. The reclining position of the rider in these vehicles makes for an enormous reduction in wind resistance permitting high speeds on flat roads. Hill climbing is difficult due to an unsuitable pedalling position, and mixing with traffic is inadvisable unless tall flags or beacons are used. Anyway such bikes are unlikely to attract a mass following in their present form even though a number of production models are now on the market. More conventional variations on the conventional bike are always in the pipeline and will quickly outstrip the topicality of this book - the important thing is for as many people as possible to recognise the way things are going. A wealth of experimentation testifies to the healthy state of cycling in general. Occasionally really useful products appear and find immediate acceptance: ultra-lightweight folding bicycles pioneered by Bickerton are enthusiastically used by many commuters nowadays since such bikes can easily be stored on trains. I have test ridden the latest - the Airframe - which has been designed by a British architect and which appears to be the best bicycle of this sort yet produced. My own particular enthusiasm is for the new all-terrain bikes, like the Ridgeback, which combine all the sophisticated accessories of a good racing bike with a really tough, light frame. In the USA bikes like this are used in downhill races run at speeds which demonstrate just how strong these machines have to be. Recently these bikes have come down into the towns and cities (one look at New York City's impressive collection of potholes tells you why) and there is every sign that the all-terrain bike will soon take its place on the urban roads in the UK as well. Whether for this purpose of simply for the exhilaration of being able to race down rutted country tracks

without losing your fillings, you should test ride an ATB if you possibly can.

The least competitive individual will often respond vigorously to being overtaken by another cyclist - private duels worthy of the Tour de France are fought daily by commuting cyclists, all desperately trying to be the first past Tescos. It's quite easy, then, to understand why all manner of competitive cycling events are arranged and well-attended. Criteriums - races in which a few street blocks are cordoned off to form a circuit - are exciting to watch and have the extra advantage of being a show brought to town. They are particularly popular in France despite being preceded by assorted civic entertainments involving processions and men with megaphones. Time trials, six-day indoor events, the Milk Race and of course the Tour de France, all have their following and the outsider needs only to be made aware of the often quite complex strategies involved in these various events, to become hooked.

TV is beginning to give competitive cycling more coverage and seems likely to awaken a much more widespread interest than ever before, if the outside broadcasts remain under the control of the British networks. European coverage, taken as it comes by the BBC or IBA too often baffles even the commentators and does nothing to explain the sport.

Another type of competition, usually appealing to the loner, involves pitting yourself against mileages which read like telephone numbers. These odysseys are often later documented in magazines by the cyclists concerned who quite naturally want to leave a more permanent record of their achievements than an ink line on a map. For the less ambitious the annual London to Brighton cycle run offers a pleasant introduction to the concept of a longish trip with a destination at the end of it. The wide range of abilities encompassed by the trip means that no one need be daunted and the event can be the starting point for some cyclist to join a club or go on group runs which happen to satisfy his social and cycling requirements.

Other directions? Well, I've indicated a few of the directions that the keen cyclist might like to consider going. You may, like me, find that just by combining a bike with your life style an enormous amount of enjoyment is to be had. Inevitably you will end up wanting more than one bike. Whilst a good bike can be pressed into all kinds of service it's nice to have exactly the machine you want for a given occasion - a super-lightweight one for fast weekend sprints and a well-equipped one for carrying heavy loads and running a dynamo. The choice is yours and will depend on your preferences.

You may feel that the cyclist is still not being afforded the rights and facilities he deserves. You would be right and if you feel strongly about it you may want to join or form a pressure group. My own feeling is that when bikes become as fully established as they now must, then it will be the able-bodied non-biker who will constantly be asked why he doesn't cycle. And once that happens then more considerate treatment for the cyclist will be inevitable; whole committees will cycle to work and as a result will make decisions of a more enlightened kind - at least as far as bikes are concerned. The only question is when this kind of situation will come about and the answer, I suppose, is about ten years after public opinion has shifted forcibly away from the poor-man's-transport syndrome. Things are moving that way, but only more and more cyclists with good machines and an intelligent interest in the bicycle and its possibilities will finally tip the balance. Petitions and well-argued cases go so far, but millions of people on bicycles go further.

In a recent magazine interview, Miles Kington, the notable wit and columnist, put forward his theory about inventions. He said "Things tend to get invented in the wrong order. Because the car came after the bicycle people think it's better. If the bike had come after the car they'd say 'What a great idea!'" It didn't, but it is.

Useful Addresses

London to Brighton
Bike Events, P.O. Box 75, Bath, Avon.

International Human Powered Vehicle Association
P.O. Box 2068, Seal Beach, CA90740, U.S.A.

Recommended dealers

This list is by no means exhaustive, but those listed are known to be reputable dealers in their respective areas.

Avon

Avon Valley Bike Hire
Railway Place
Bath

Fred Baker Cycles
144 Cheltenham Road
Bristol BS6 5RL

Johns Bikes
1 Cleveland Place East
London Road
Bath

Overbury's Cycles
138 Ashley Road
Bristol BS6 5PA

Les Wilkins Cycles Ltd
10 Walliscote Road
Weston Super Mare

Berkshire

Stonham Cycles
23 Parkside Road
Thatcham RG13 4BJ

Stows
6 Windsor Road
Slough SL1 2EJ

Bucks

Phil Corley Cycles
Neath Hill Local Centre
Neath Hill
Milton Keynes

Cycle Care Ltd
216 Desborough Road
High Wycombe HP11 2TF

Cambridgeshire

Ben Hayward & Son
69 Trumpington Street
Cambridge

Howes Cycles
104 Regent Street
Cambridge CB2 1DP

YHA Cambridge
6/7 Bridge Street
Cambridge CB2 1VA

Channel Islands

Wheels Ltd
Its House
Les Banques
St Peter Port
Guernsey

Cheshire

Davies Bros Ltd
6/8 Cuppin Street
Chester

Doug Hartley
100/104 Ashley Road
Hale
Altrincham

Cleveland

Colin Armstrong Cycles
22/24 Princess Road
Middlesborough

Gloucestershire

Cycology Ltd
42 Goldsmith Road
Coronation Square
Cheltenham

A Williams Co (Cyc) Ltd
8/14 Portland Street
Cheltenham

Cornwall

Carter & Hall
119/121 New Road
Portsmouth

Lyoness Repairs
Cross Street
Penzance

Derbyshire

Chesterfield Cycle Centre
Brimington Road North
Chesterfield

Mercian Cycles Ltd
7 Shardlow Road
Alvaston
Derby

Devon

Devon Cycles
2 Frankfort Gate
Plymouth PL1 1QD

Colin Lewis
5/7 Manor Corner
Preston
Paignton

Norton Cycles
141 Fore Street
Exeter

Dorset

Geo Dixon Cycles
244 Charminster Road
Charminster
Bournemouth

Ken Prescott
985 Christchurch Road
Boscombe
Bournemouth

Shepherds Cycles
319 Ashley Road
Parkstone
Poole

Co Durham

Denton Cycles (Newcastle) Ltd
177 Westgate Rd
Newcastle upon Tyne NE1 4HA

Dave Heron Cycles
6 Neville Street
Durham City

M Steel
5 Salters Road
Gosforth
Newcastle upon Tyne NE3 1DH

Chris Thompson Cycles
29 High Northgate
Darlington
Durham

Essex

B J Cycles
108 Ardleigh Green Road
Hornchurch

Bates of Westcliff
479 London Road
Westcliff on Sea

Buckley Saxon Cycles Ltd
St James Street
Castle Hedingham
Nr Halstead

Colchester Cycle Stores
Old Cameo Cinema
St Johns Street
Colchester

Hetchins Bike Shop
117/119 Hamstel Road
Southend-on-Sea

Rory o'Brien
134 North Stret
Romford

Swallow Frames/Cycles
2 Stannetts
Laindon North Trading Estate
Laindon

The Cycle and Toy Centre
New Street
Chelmsford

Hants

Fleet Cycles
181A Fleet Road
Fleet

Jim Guard Cycles
120 MacNaughton Road
Southampton

Renhams Cycles
3 St Denys Road
Portswood
Southampton SO2 1GN

Rotrax Cycles
132 Shirley Road
Freemantle
Southampton

Southampton Bike Centre
Unit 16
East Street Shopping Centre
Southampton

Herts

Ashblue Ltd
14/16 Newtown Road
Bishops Stortford

Jim Boyce Bikes
The Wynd
Letchworth SG6 3EL

Nigel Dean Cycles
94 Victoria Street
St Albans

C J Frost & Son
95 Walsworth Road
Hitchin SG4 9SU

J A Moore
12/13 St Albans Rd East
Hatfield

Ryan Cycles
Unit E2
The Maltings
Sawbridgenorth

Humberside

Ken Ellerker
275/277 Chanterlands Ave
Hull HU5 4DL

Cliff Pratt Ltd
84 Spring Bank
Hull HU3 1AA

Alan Whitehead Cycles
Chichester House
School Green Road
Freshwater
Isle of Wight

Ireland

R S Rowen & Sons
14 Palmerston Place
Broadstone
Dublin 7

Northern Ireland

Dave Kane Cycles
309 Upper Newtownards Road
Ballyhackamore
Belfast

DMD Cycles Ltd
18 Grafton Street
Cork

Kent

Ken Bird Cycles
35/37 High Street
Green Street Green
Nr Orpington

Cyclewise
140 Ashford Road
Bearstead
Maidstone

Geoff Wiles Cycles
47 Cuxton Road
Stroud

Lancashire

Alan Dent Cycles
4 China Street
Lancaster

Freckleton Cycles
49 Lytham Road
Freckleton
Preston PR4 IAB

M K Cycles
95/97 Tonge Moor Road
Bolton

J Partington
11 Great Moor Street
Bolton

Ribble Cycles
6/8 Watery Lane
Ashton
Preston

Keith Townsend
107 St Andrews Road North
St Annes On Sea

Warlands Cycles
20/22 King Street
Blackburn
Lancs BB2 2DH

Leicestershire

Beacon Cycles Ltd
30 High Street
Loughborough

Julie's Cycle Shop
216 Clarendon Park Road
Leicester

Leedhams
3 Narborough Road
Leicester

London

E G Bates
589/591 Barking Road
Plaistow
London E13 9EZ

Beta Bikes
275 Westend Lane
London NW6 1QS

Bike UK Ltd
York Building
Strand
London WC2

Birds of Colindale
273 Edgware Road
Colindale
London NW9

Camden Bikes Ltd
3 Camden Road
Camden Town
London NW1 9LG

E Chamberlaine Ltd
71/77 Kentish Town Road
London NW1

Condor Cycles
144/8 Grays Inn Road
London WC1

Covent Garden Cycles
41 Shorts Gardens
London WC2

Edwards Camberwell Ltd
223/225 Camberwell Road
London SE5

F W Evans
77/79 The Cut
London SE1

Fudge Cycles
176 High Road
Chiswick
London W4

Fulham Cycle Store
921 Fulham Road
London SW6

Pat Hanlon Cycles
77 Bowes Road
Palmers Green
London N13

Harrods
Knighstbridge
London SW1

W F Holdsworth
132 Lower Richmond Road
Putney
London SW15

London Bicycle Co
41 Floral Street
London WC2

London Bicycle Co
53/55 Pimlico Road
London SW1

Oscroft Brothers
191 Woodhouse Road
Friern Barnet
London N12 9AY

Pedal Palace
59 Chalton Street
London NW1

Harry Perry Cycles
8 Wellington Street
Woolwich
London SE18

Phoenix Cycles
120 Stanstead Road
London SE23

Riders Cycles
490 Caladonian Road
London N7

Roberts Cycle
87 Penge Road
Annerley
London SE20

Robins Bikes
520/522 Forest Road
Walthamstow
London E17

Saviles Cycle Stores Ltd
97/99 Battersea Rise
London SW11 1HW

Shorter Rochford
65/67 Woodhouse Road
Finchley
London N12

Brian Simpson
116 Malden Road
Kentish Town
London NW5

G W Stratton
101 East Hill
Wandsworth
London SW18

Stuart Bikes
309/311 Horn Lane
Acton
London W3

Stuarts Cycles
1 Ascot Parade
Clapham Park Road
London SW4

Swift Cycles
18 Dartmouth Road
Forest Hill
London SE23 3XU

Tracks Sports Ltd
42/44 Clapham High Street
London SW4

Y H A Services Ltd
14 Southampton Street
London WC2E 7HY

Youngs Cycles
290 Lee High Road
Lewisham
London SE13

Manchester

Didsbury Cycles
698 Wimslow Road
Didsbury
Manchster
M20 ODN

Harry Hall Cycles
30/32 Cathedral Street
Manchester
M4 3EY

CDC Robson Cycles
281/283 Barlow Moor Road
Chorlton-Cum-Hardy
Manchester

YHA Manchester
166 Deansgate
Manchester M33 5E

Merseyside

Heswall Bicycles
64 Telegraph Road
Heswall
Wirral
L60 OAG

The 'K' Cycle and Hardware Store
1186 Newchester
Eastham
Wirral

Quinn Bros Cycles
383/5 Edge Lane
Liverpool
L7 9LQ

Walvale Cycles
58/60 Walton Vale
Liverpool
L9 2BU

Middlesex

Mal Rees Ltd
13 Coldharbour Lane
Hayes

Rohans Cycles
451/455 Rayner's Lane
Pinner

Midlands

John Atkins
140 Far Gosford Street
Coventry
West Midlands

Bearwood Cycles
430/432 Bearwood Road
Warley
Birmingham B66 4EY

Tommy Godwin Cycles
10 Silver Street
Kings Heath
Birmingham 14

O W Hopkins
1539 Stafford Road
Hall Green
Birmingham

Priory Cycles
1556 Stratford Road
Birmingham B28 9HA

Tower Cycles
168/178 Gravelly Lane
Erdington
Birmingham B23 55N

Fred Williams Cyc Ltd
No 1 Cleveland Road
Wolverhampton
West Midlands

YHA Birmingham
92/98 Corporation Street
Birmingham B4

Norfolk

John Borwell Cycles
82A Knowsley Road
Norwich
NR3 4PS

Northants

Oakley Cycles
86 Lutterworth Road
Northampton

Supabikes
48 Kinglsey Park Terrace
Northampton
NN2 7HH

Northumberland

Sanders Cycles
71 Station Road
Ashington
Northumberland

Nottinghamshire

Castle Cycles
15/17 Boar Lane
Newark
NG24 1HH

Langdale Lightweight
459 Westdale Lane
Mapperley
Nottingham NG3

Olympic Cycles
43 Radford Road
Hyson Green
Nottingham

Sid Standard
35/37 Chilwell Road
Beeston
Nottingham

Oxon

Broadribbs
6 Lincoln House
Market Street
Oxford

Dentons
294 Banbury Road
Oxford
OX2 7ED

Dentons (Witney)
1 High Street
Witney

Walton Street Cycles
78 Walton Street
Oxford

Scotland

Aberdeen Cycle Centre
King Street
Aberdeen

James Anderson & Sons
46/50 Rosemount Viaduct
Aberdeen AB1

Autoparts
52 Princes Street
Thurso
Caithness

The Bicycle Shop
9 West Richmond Street
Edinburgh EH8 9EF

Billy Bilsland Cycles
176 Selpmarket
Glasgow G1 5LA

Bishopleasure Cycles
79 Kenneth Street
Inverness

City Cycles (Edinburgh)
87 Slateford Road
Edinburgh EH11 1QR

Dales Cycles Ltd
26/30 Maryhill Road
Glasgow G20 7PZ

Edinburgh Cycle Hire
8 Alvanley Terrace
Whitehouse Loan
Edinburgh

Ghyllside Cycles
The Slack
Ambleside
Cumbria LA22 9DQ

Sandy Gilchrist Cycles
1 Cadzow Place
Abbey Hill
Edinmburgh EH7

A Junner & Co Ltd
79 South Street
Elgin

W & R McDonald
26 Morrison Street
Edinburgh EH3

New Bike Shop
Market Place
Workington
Cumbria CA14 4AX

J R Nicholson
2 Forfar Road
Dundee

Ken Stubbs
7 St Barnabas Road
Linthorpe
Cleveland
TS6 6JR

Thornton Cycles
23 Castle Street
Inverness IV23 DU

Robin Williamson Cycles
26 Hamilton Place
Edinburgh EH3 5AU

Stewart Wilson Cycles
35 Baker Street
Stirling

Somerset

P D E Cycles
72 Wessex Road
Yeovil

Staffordshire

Henry Burton Cycles
3 Mill Street
Stafford

Brian Rourke Cycles
221 Waterloo Road
Burslem
Stoke on Trent
ST6 3ES

Roy Swinnerton
69 Victoria Road
Fenton
Stoke on Trent

Suffolk

Buck Cycles
211 Clapgate Lane
Ipswich
IP3 ORF

Surrey

Allin Cycles
57/59 White Horse Road
Croydon

Geoffrey Butler Cycles
9 South End
Croydon

B Finch & Sons
41 & 43 Bell Street
Reigate
Surrey
RH2 7AQ

Kingston Cycles
48 Richmond Road
Kingston

Pearsons
126 High Street
Sutton

Pedal Pushers
72a & 73 Woodbridge Road
Guildford
GU1 4QH

Richmond Cycles
36 Hill Street
Richmond on Thames

Surrey Cycles
56 High Street
Camberley
GU15 3RS

Walden Cycles Ltd
136 London Road
Kingston upon Thames

Woking Cycles
1 Guildford Road
Woking

YHA Staines
133/135 High Street
Staines TW18 4PD

Sussex

C & N Supplies
31 Broadway
Crawley
Sussex

Cooks for Cycles
Portland Road
Hove
Sussex

Cycle Revival
Multon Hall Hill
Heathfield
East Sussex
TN21 8NG

M & J Cycles
4 Beaconsfield Parade
Brighton
BN1 6DL

Horsham Cycles
53 East Street
Horsham
RH12 1HR

Rayment Cycles
14 Circus Parade
New England Road
Brighton

John Spooner Cycles
21 Farm Road
Worthing
West Sussex

Wales

Reg Braddick & Sons
59/61 Broadway
Cardiff
CF2 1XJ

Greenstiles Cycle Workshop
Tremount Road
Llandrindod Wells
Powys

Mikes Bikes
Field Street
Upper Bangor
Gwynedd

YHA Cardiff
131 Woodville Road
Cathays
Cardiff

Warwickshire

C H Smith
26 High Street
Leamington Spa
CV 31

Wiltshire

Haines & Son
8/10 Water Lane
Salisbury

Worcestershire

Brian Coombes Cycles
98 Widemarsh Street
Hereford

Speeds Cycles
72 Birmingham Road
Bromsgrove

Yorkshire

Allens Cycle Centre
23 Barnsley Road
Wombwell
Barnsley

Branch's
Bridge Gate
Hebden Bridge
West Yorkshire

Tony Butterworth
88/90 Catchbar Lane
Sheffield
S6 1TA

Daves Bike Shop
73 Raglan Road
Leeds 2

Ellis-Briggs Ltd
18 Otley Rd
Shipley

J R J Cycles
148 Harehills Lane
Leeds LS8 5BD

Keith Lambert Cycles
108 Main Street
Bingley
West Yorkshire
BD16 2JH

Langsett Cycles
182/192 Infirmary Road
Sheffield
S6 3DH

Rough Stuff Fellowship
1 Wedderburn Road
Harrogate
HG2 7QH

C S Russell (York) Ltd
Clifford Street
York
Y01 1RG

Settle Cycles
Duke Street
Settle
North Yorkshire

Bob Trotter
18 Monkgate
York

Mike Walker Cycles
18 Water Street
Skipton
North Yorkshire

Woodrup Cycles
345/347 Kirkstall Road
Leeds 4

York Cycle Works
16 Lawrence Street
York

NOTES